Texas Rules of Form

The Greenbook

Texas Rules of Form

The Greenbook

SIXTEENTH EDITION

Texas Law Review

Copies of *Texas Rules of Form: The Greenbook* are distributed by:

The University of Texas School of Law

Attn: Publications
727 E. Dean Keeton St.
Austin, Texas 78705

(512) 232-1149
publications@law.utexas.edu
https://texaslawreview.org/ordering/

To order a copy of *Texas Rules of Form: The Greenbook,* please visit https://texaslawreview.org/ordering/.

Copy Price: $25.00 each for orders under 25; $20.00 each for orders of 25 or more. Texas residents please include 8.25% tax.

For correspondence about the content of *Texas Rules of Form: The Greenbook,* please email greenbook@texaslrev.com.

Published under license by the University of Texas at Austin School of Law, 727 E. Dean Keeton St., Austin, TX 78705-3299.

First edition published 1966. Sixteenth edition 2025.

Printed in the United States of America

ISBN: 979-8-218-73999-7

The sixteenth edition of *Texas Rules of Form: The Greenbook* was printed in Hanover, Pennsylvania. The pages were marked up and proofed by the sixteenth edition editorial staff. The text was designed by Drew Synan and composed in Hoefler & Frere-Jones's Sentinel and Ideal Sans. The cover was designed by David Singer.

Contents

Foreword

Citations are all about being credible and reliable. Although good citation form won't win over many readers, poor form will assuredly put off those who prize accuracy. So if you're a graduate student, you must know Turabian's *Manual for Writers of Term Papers, Theses, and Dissertations*. If you're a scholar in the humanities, you must know your *MLA Style Manual*. If you're on the editorial side of book publishing, you must know your *Chicago Manual of Style*. And if you're a Texas lawyer, you must know *The Greenbook*.

Published by the *Texas Law Review*, and now in its sixteenth edition, *The Greenbook* authoritatively guides scholars and practitioners through the thickets of citing Texas legal authorities. If you learned the basics years ago, spend some time with this new edition: you'll be surprised (as I was) at the extent of what you've forgotten. If you're learning this stuff for the first time, try not to be intimidated by it. You may have to try hard, but it's worth the effort.

If you're writing about Texas law and hope to seem to know what you're doing, you'll need to follow the guidance here. Many readers—perfectly decent and humane people in other respects—won't give your writing a serious look if you don't.

Bryan A. Garner
LawProse, Inc.
Dallas, Texas

Introduction

This edition of the *Texas Rules of Form*, better known as *The Greenbook*, is the first to be published since the creation of the Texas Business Court and the Fifteenth Court of Appeals. In light of these landmark developments, we felt it was essential to collaborate with the Texas legal community at every stage of our editing process.

At the outset of our edit, we surveyed the public for recommendations to strengthen *The Greenbook*. We translated these recommendations into provisionary rules and held our first public comment period, allowing the Texas legal community to respond to our proposed changes. The feedback we received was instrumental in refining and finalizing this edition.

Editing *The Greenbook* was a labor of love not only for our staff, but also for the many volunteers who shared their thoughts with us. Every change featured in this edition reflects the insights and dedication of those who care deeply about the practice of law in Texas. (For a list of these revisions, please see "Changes" on page 1.)

On behalf of all the editors at the *Texas Law Review* and the volunteers who participated in our editing process, thank you for purchasing the sixteenth edition of *The Greenbook*. We hope it serves you well.

Matt Saletta
Texas Law Review
Editor-in-Chief, Vol. 104

Editorial Staff

Editors

Matt Saletta, *Editor-in-Chief*

Natalie Robinson, *Managing Editor*

Jiayi "Lily" Li, *Administrative Editor*

Contributors

Brandon Charnov

Brian Murphy

Collin Lawrence

Rehm Maham

Sean Steck

And thank you to Teri Gaus, *Texas Law Review*'s phenomenal Editorial Assistant.

Changes in the Sixteenth Edition

- This edition of *The Greenbook* provides guidance for citation to cases from the Fifteenth Court of Appeals and the Texas Business Court. See **Rule 4** & **Rule 7.1.1**.
- This edition of *The Greenbook* has removed the requirement to designate "mem. op." and "per curiam" for civil cases. See **Rule 4.1.2**.
- This edition standardizes the abbreviation for "county" in line with national conventions. See **Rule 7.2**.
- This edition eliminates the "Ann." designation requirement for annotated reprints of codified statutes. See **Rule 10.2.1**.
- Historically, *The Greenbook* has only allowed citation to statutes and session laws featured on commercial databases. The sixteenth edition allows users to cite from databases hosted by the Texas Legislative Council and the Legislative Reference Library of Texas. See **Rule 10.5**.
- This edition of *The Greenbook* provides detailed guidance regarding citation to gubernatorial proclamations and expands the range for sources from which proclamations may be cited. See **Rule 14.7.2**.
- This edition of *The Greenbook* illustrates how to format pincites in citations to Attorney General Opinions and Secretary of State Advisory Opinions. See **Rule 15**.
- Lastly, this edition of *The Greenbook* requires greater specificity for cites to Texas Administrative Code in order to make these sources more accessible to users relying on public databases. See **Rule 16.1.1**.

PART I
TYPEFACE CONVENTIONS

Chapter 1 presents the simplified conventions that practitioners traditionally use for briefs and legal memoranda.

Law Review Typeface Conventions

In-Text Citations—*Italicize* case names and titles of publications, speeches, or articles. All other material appears in roman type. Full citations should not appear in the text of law review articles.

Footnote Citations—Three typefaces are used for citations in law review footnotes: roman, *italics*, and LARGE AND SMALL CAPITALS. For more information on typeface conventions consult *The Bluebook*.

1 Briefs and Legal Memoranda

Two typefaces traditionally appear in briefs, memoranda, and similar material: roman and *italics*. The examples in *The Greenbook* follow this typeface convention, but the fifteenth edition permits the usage of LARGE AND SMALL CAPITALS for stylistic purposes. This change was also adopted in the twentieth edition of *The Bluebook*. See Bluepages B2.

To distinguish citations from text in legal briefs and memoranda, the following material should be *italicized*:

1.1 Introductory Signals and Explanatory Phrases

Signals used to introduce authorities are *italicized*:

Accord *Compare . . . , with*

A comma that follows the signal is not italicized, but commas within signals are *italicized*:

See, e.g., *E.g.,*

1.2 Cases

In briefs and legal memoranda, *italicize* case names. Reporters, jurisdictional information, and writ or petition histories are in roman typeface:

Beckendorff v. Harris-Galveston Coastal Subsidence Dist., 558 S.W.2d 75 (Tex. App.—Houston [14th Dist.] 1977, writ ref'd n.r.e.).

Phrases used in subsequent history, except writ or petition treatment, or in identifying secondary sources are *italicized*:

rev'd on other grounds *cert. denied,*

noted in *cited with approval in*

Note that their accompanying commas are usually not italicized. The one exception to this rule is the subsequent history phrase "*leave granted, mand. denied,*" which is specific to the writ of mandamus as practiced in Texas. The comma between "*granted*" and "*mand.*" is *italicized*:

leave granted, mand. denied

1.3 Publications

Italicize book titles and titles of articles from periodicals or newspapers. Case names appearing in a title are not italicized. Names of authors and names of periodicals and newspapers appear in roman type:

Page Keeton & Marshall S. Shapo, *Products and the Consumer: Deceptive Practices* (1972).

Miriam Galston, *Lobbying and the Public Interest: Rethinking the Internal Revenue Code's Treatment of Legislative Activities,* 71 Texas L. Rev. 1269 (1993).

Randall Kennedy, *Justice Murphy's Concurrence in* Oyama v. California*: Cussing Out Racism,* 74 Texas L. Rev. 1245 (1996).

Anne Belli, *Judges May Have Bailiffs Check for Weapons,* Dallas Morning News, July 18, 1992, at 34A.

1.4 Cross-References and Short Forms

Supra, infra, and *id.* are all *italicized.* The commas following them should appear in roman type. "Hereinafter" is also written in roman type:

See supra text accompanying notes 147–52.

See infra notes 12–15 and accompanying text.

The Texas Deceptive Trade Practice–Consumer Protection Act: Hearings on Tex. H.B. 417 Before the House Comm. on Bus. & Indus., 63d Leg., R.S., 26–28 (May 21, 1973) [hereinafter *DTPA Hearings*].

1.5 Stylistic Purposes

Words may be *italicized* for stylistic purposes to show emphasis, but this device is used only when the sentence cannot be structured in a way that makes the emphasis apparent. See generally *Texas Law Review Manual on Usage & Style* 4.01 (Texas Law Review Ass'n ed., 15th ed. 2020).

Foreign words not incorporated into common usage appear in *italics*. There is a strong presumption that commonly used legal Latin phrases have been incorporated into common usage and thus are not italicized. See generally *The Bluebook* Rule 7(b).

In direct quotations words should retain the typeface found in the original source unless a parenthetical notation of the change is appended.

1.6 Everything Else

Everything else—including statutes, rules, legislative histories, administrative materials, and unpublished works—is customarily written in roman type.

PART II
TEXAS CASES

Procedure

The route a case takes through the appeals process depends on whether the case is civil or criminal.

- Nearly all cases decided in the trial courts on or after September 1, 1981, may be appealed only to the Texas Courts of Appeals (formerly the Texas Courts of Civil Appeals).
- Civil cases decided in the courts of appeals may be appealed to the Texas Supreme Court by filing a petition for review.
- Criminal cases may be appealed to the Texas Court of Criminal Appeals by filing a petition for review. In addition, the Court of Criminal Appeals may, on its own motion, review decisions of the courts of appeals in criminal matters.
- Criminal cases involving the imposition of the death penalty are subject to automatic review by the Texas Court of Criminal Appeals, bypassing the courts of appeals.

Consult *The Bluebook* Rule 10 for case citation rules not covered in Part II.

2 Texas Supreme Court

Format Guide

Current Cases	*Jupiter Oil Co. v. Snow*, 819 S.W.2d 466, 467 (Tex. 1991).
Short Form	*Jupiter Oil Co.*, 819 S.W.2d at 467.
Recent Decisions	*City of Keller v. Wilson*, No. 02-1012, 2005 WL 1366509, at *1–2 (Tex. June 10, 2005).
Short Form	*City of Keller*, 2005 WL 1366509, at *1–2.

2.1 Current Cases

2.1.1 Basic Citation Format

Citations to decisions of the Texas Supreme Court include the case name, a citation to the volume and page of the *South Western Reporter*, the specific page containing the cited material, and a parenthetical indicating the name of the court ("Tex.") and the year of decision. Include subsequent history if appropriate (see **Rule 2.2**):

HEB Ministries, Inc. v. Texas Higher Educ. Coordinating Bd., 235 S.W.3d 627, 646 (Tex. 2007).

Case names should be cited in accordance with *The Bluebook* Rule 10.2.

2.1.2 Recent Decisions—Slip Opinions, Electronic Citations, and the *Texas Supreme Court Journal*

Cases that have not yet appeared in the advance sheets of the *South Western Reporter* must be cited to an electronic medium if possible. Such citations must include the case name, the cause number, a citation to LEXIS or Westlaw if using one of these services (see *The Bluebook* Rule 10.8), the specific page containing the cited material, and a parenthetical including the name of the court ("Tex.") and the exact date of the decision:

Am. K-9 Detection Servs., LLC v. Freeman, No. 15-0932, 2018 WL 3207134, at *3 (Tex. June 29, 2018).

(a) **Citation to Paginated Opinion on Court Website.** If citing to a paginated version of an opinion on the Court's website, follow the citation rules provided in **Rule 2.1.2(a)**, but include the page number after the "slip op." designation:

City of Keller v. Wilson, No. 02-1012, slip op. at 2 (Tex. June 10, 2005), *available at* http://www.search.txcourts.gov/historical/2005/jun/021012.pdf.

(b) **Citing to a Case Generally.** When citing a case generally, there is no need to include a "slip op." designation:

See generally City of Keller v. Wilson, No. 02-1012 (Tex. June 10, 2005), *available at* http://www.search.txcourts.gov/historical/2005/jun/021012.pdf.

(c) ***Texas Supreme Court Journal.*** Cases not yet appearing in the *South Western Reporter* advance sheets can be cited to the *Texas Supreme Court Journal* (abbreviated "Tex. Sup. Ct. J."). Such a citation must include the case name, a citation to the volume and page of the *Texas Supreme Court Journal*, the specific page containing the cited material, and a parenthetical with the exact date of the decision. The court designation ("Tex.") is omitted as redundant. A parallel citation to an electronic medium, such as LEXIS or Westlaw, is also included (see *The Bluebook* Rule 10.8):

Texas Dep't of State Health Servs. v. Crown Distrib., 65 Tex. Sup. Ct. J. 1630, 1630, 2022 WL 2283170, at *1 (June 24, 2022).

2.2 Disposition by the Supreme Court of the United States and Other Subsequent History

Full citation to a case *must* include any disposition made by the Supreme Court of the United States, *except that* denials of certiorari for opinions over two years old should be omitted unless particularly relevant:

Chapman v. King Ranch, Inc., 118 S.W.3d 742 (Tex. 2003), *cert. denied*, 541 U.S. 1030 (2004).

Do not cite subsequent history other than Supreme Court of the United States dispositions unless relevant to the point for which the case is cited. For example, the denial of a rehearing and the history of a case on remand generally are not cited.

2.3 *Texas Reports*

From 1846 until 1962, opinions of the Texas Supreme Court were published in an official reporter, the *Texas Reports*. Between 1886 and 1962, opinions were published in both the *Texas Reports* and an unofficial reporter, the *South Western Reporter*. The *Texas Reports* ceased publication in 1962.

2.3.1 Cases—1846 to 1886

Opinions issued during this period are available only in the *Texas Reports*. See **Appendix A** for information on citing these cases and earlier cases from the Republic of Texas.

2.3.2 Cases—1886 to 1962

Parallel citations to both reporters are not generally required in either legal memoranda or court documents. If, however, a court's local rule requires a parallel citation, citations should include the case name, a citation to the volume and page of the official *Texas Reports*, the specific page of the *Texas Reports* containing the cited material, a parallel citation to the *South Western Reporter*, and a parenthetical including the year of decision (the court designation ("Tex.") is omitted as redundant):

Jones v. Strayhorn, 159 Tex. 421, 423, 321 S.W.2d 290, 292 (1959).

Strayhorn, 159 Tex. at 423, 321 S.W.2d at 292.

3 Texas Court of Criminal Appeals

Format Guide

Current Cases	*Cantu v. State,* 939 S.W.2d 627, 631 (Tex. Crim. App. 1997).
Short Form	*Cantu,* 939 S.W.2d at 628.
Recent Decisions	*Cooper v. State,* No. 1100-99, 2001 WL 321579, at *2–3 (Tex. Crim. App. Apr. 4, 2001).
Short Form	*Cooper,* 2001 WL 321579, at *2–3.

3.1 Current Cases

3.1.1 Basic Citation Format

► Practice Tip

Unpublished opinions of the Texas Court of Criminal Appeals have no precedential value and must not be cited as authority by counsel or by a court. If a citation is required for other purposes, it should follow this form:

Massoth v. State, No. 14-03-00605-CR, 2004 WL 1381027, at *1 (Tex. App.—Houston [14th Dist.] June 22, 2004, pet. ref'd) (mem. op., not designated for publication), *habeas corpus granted in part sub nom. Ex parte Massoth,* No. AP-75215, 2005 WL 1774115, at *1 (Tex. Crim. App. July 27, 2005) (per curiam) (not designated for publication).

All citations to Texas Court of Criminal Appeals cases since August 1962 must include the case name, a citation to the volume and page of the *South Western Reporter*, the specific page containing the cited material, a parenthetical indicating the court name ("Tex. Crim. App.") and the year of decision, and subsequent history, if appropriate (see **Rule 8.2** for proper citation of subsequent history):

Cantu v. State, 939 S.W.2d 627, 629 (Tex. Crim. App. 1997).

Case names should be cited in accordance with *The Bluebook* Rule 10.2.

3.1.2 Panel Opinions—1978 to 1982

From 1978 to 1982, some decisions of the Texas Court of Criminal Appeals were by a panel of the Court. Cite such panel opinions by including the designation "[Panel Op.]" in the parenthetical, immediately following the court name:

Stringer v. State, 632 S.W.2d 340, 341 (Tex. Crim. App. [Panel Op.] 1982).

Occasionally a Court of Criminal Appeals opinion is designated as "en banc." It is unnecessary to indicate this in citations to such opinions.

3.1.3 Recent Decisions—Slip Opinions and Electronic Citations

Cases that have not yet appeared in the advance sheets of the *South Western Reporter* must be cited to an electronic medium if possible. Such citations must include the case name, the cause number, a citation to LEXIS or Westlaw if using one of these services (see *The Bluebook* Rule 10.8), the specific page containing the cited material, and a parenthetical including the name of the court ("Tex. Crim. App.") and the exact date of the decision:

Cooper v. State, No. 1100-99, 2001 WL 321579, at *2 (Tex. Crim. App. Apr. 4, 2001).

(a) **Citation to Unpaginated Opinion on Court Website.** The Court of Criminal Appeals provides recent opinions on its website. When citing to an opinion provided on the Court's website, a designation "*available at*" followed by the URL should generally be provided after the court parenthetical.

When citing to a slip opinion provided in a form that does not indicate pagination, use a pinpoint citation to a paragraph or other segment that will best direct the reader to the material cited. Include the designation "slip op." before the paragraph number:

Powell v. State, No. PD-0051-05, slip op. ¶ 2 (Tex. Crim. App. Apr. 5, 2006), *available at* http://search.txcourts.gov/Case.aspx?cn=PD-0051-05&coa=coscca.

(b) Citation to Paginated Opinion on Court Website. If citing to a paginated version of an opinion on the Court's website, follow the citation rules provided in **Rule 3.1.3(a)**, but include the page number after the "slip op." designation:

Carron v. State, No. WR-88,625-01, slip op. at 2 (Tex. Crim. App. July 25, 2018), *available at* http://search.txcourts.gov/SearchMedia.aspx?MediaVersionID=b18d049b-06c1-42c9-8e30-8f970c4b9e77&coa=coscca&DT=OPINION&MediaID=71ae79d9-a57d-496c-9141-df75aca974e2.

(c) Citing to a Case Generally. When citing a case generally, the "slip op." designation may be omitted:

See generally Powell v. State, No. PD-0051-05 (Tex. Crim. App. Apr. 5, 2006), *available at* http://search.txcourts.gov/SearchMedia.aspx?MediaVersionID=7adb9776-9df3-4753-a6fb-be90a5c9f92c&coa=coscca&DT=OPINION&MediaID=f085d163-d9c2-4931-9421-72e173779bc1.

3.2 Disposition by the Supreme Court of the United States and Other Subsequent History

Full citation to a case *must* include any disposition made by the Supreme Court of the United States *except that* denials of certiorari and similar dispositions of discretionary appeals should be omitted for opinions over two years old unless directly relevant to the reason for citing the case:

Johnson v. State, 755 S.W.2d 92 (Tex. Crim. App. 1988), *aff'd*, 491 U.S. 397 (1989).

Ex parte Smith, 185 S.W.3d 455, 457 (Tex. Crim. App. 2006), *rev'd sub nom. Smith v. Texas*, 550 U.S. 297, 300 (2007).

Do not cite subsequent history other than Supreme Court of the United States dispositions unless relevant to the point for which the case is cited. For example, the denial of a rehearing and the history of a case on remand generally are not cited.

3.3 *Texas Criminal Reports*

From 1892 until 1962, opinions of the Texas Court of Criminal Appeals were published in an official reporter, *Texas Criminal Reports*, and the *South Western Reporter*. *Texas Criminal Reports* ceased publication in 1962.

Parallel citations to both reporters are not generally required in either legal memoranda or court documents. If, however, a court's local rule requires a parallel citation, citations should include the case name, a citation to the volume and page of the official *Texas Criminal Reports*, the specific page of the *Texas Criminal Reports* containing the cited material, a parallel citation to the *South Western Reporter*, and a parenthetical including the year of decision (the court designation ("Tex. Crim. App.") is omitted as redundant):

Full Citation: *Laredo v. State*, 155 Tex. Crim. 183, 184, 232 S.W.2d 852, 853 (1950).

Short Citation: *Laredo*, 155 Tex. Crim. at 184, 232 S.W.2d at 853.

Historical Note

In 1892, the Legislature replaced the old Texas Court of Appeals with the present Texas Court of Criminal Appeals and limited the new court's jurisdiction to criminal cases. For information on citations to the old Texas Court of Appeals see **Appendix B**. The official reporter, *Texas Court of Appeals Reports*, was renamed the *Texas Criminal Reports*, but the volumes continued in the same numerical sequence, beginning with volume thirty-one. Although some variation in numbering may occur with different bound sets, it is correct to cite all volumes beginning with volume thirty-one as "Tex. Crim."

4 Courts of Appeals

Format Guide

Current Cases	*Cooper v. Tex. Dep't of Human Res.*, 691 S.W.2d 807, 808 (Tex. App.—Austin 1985, writ ref'd n.r.e.).
Short Form	*Cooper*, 691 S.W.2d at 808.
Memorandum Opinions	*Richardson v. Kays*, No. 02-03241-CV, 2003 WL 22457054, at *2 (Tex. App.—Fort Worth Oct. 30, 2003, no pet.) (per curiam) (mem. op.).
Short Form	*Richardson*, 2003 WL 22457054, at *2.
Opinions Not Designated for Publication	*Young v. State*, No. 10-02-00186-CR, 2003 WL 22023670, at *2 (Tex. App.—Waco Aug. 27, 2003, no pet.) (mem. op., not designated for publication).
Recent Decisions	*Klentzman v. Brady*, No. 01-11-00765-CV, 2013 WL 5655845, at *2 (Tex. App.—Houston [1st Dist.] Oct. 17, 2013, no pet. h.).

4.1 Current Cases—1981 to Date

4.1.1 Basic Citation Form

Cite all reported courts of appeals cases decided on or after September 1, 1981, only to the *South Western Reporter*. A complete citation must contain the case name; a citation to the volume and page of the *South Western Reporter*; the specific page containing the cited material;

a parenthetical, including the name of the court ("Tex. App."), an em dash (there is no space on either side of the em dash) followed by the city in which that court is located, if applicable, (**Rule 4.3**), the date, the writ history or petition history (**Rules 4.4** and **4.5**), and a notation of interlocutory orders, if appropriate (**Rule 4.7**); parenthetical information regarding weight of authority, if appropriate (**Rule 4.1.2**); and any subsequent history (**Rule 4.6**):

Cooper v. Tex. Dep't of Human Res., 691 S.W.2d 807, 808 (Tex. App.—Austin 1985, writ ref'd n.r.e.).

IPCO-G. & C. Joint Venture v. A.B. Chance Co., 65 S.W.3d 252, 254 (Tex. App.—Houston [1st Dist.] 2001, pet. denied).

Reames v. BNP Commercial Props., Ltd., No. 13-05-631-CV, 2006 WL 1030121, at *1 (Tex. App.—Corpus Christi Apr. 20, 2006, no pet.) (per curiam) (mem. op.).

Case names should be cited in accordance with *The Bluebook* Rule 10.2.

▸ Practice Tip

Both *The Bluebook* and *The Greenbook* distinguish between three types of dashes: the em dash, the en dash, and the hyphen. For more on how and when to use which particular dash see generally *Texas Law Review Manual on Usage & Style* 1.27–1.33.

4.1.2 Parenthetical Information Regarding Weight of Authority

In both criminal and civil cases, a majority of the justices who consider the case must determine whether the opinion will be signed by a justice or will be per curiam. These opinions must also be designated as either an "Opinion" or a "Memorandum Opinion." For a definition of "Memorandum Opinion" see generally Texas Rules of Appellate Procedure 47.4.

For general rules on weight-of-authority parentheticals see *The Bluebook* Rule 10.6.1.

(a) Current Civil Cases. As of January 1, 2003, the courts of appeals must publish an opinion in every civil case, and all cases have precedential value. (When citing pre-2003 opinions, consult **Rule 4.1.2(c)**.)

For cases designated "per curiam," a parenthetical so indicating ("per curiam") may be included after the court parenthetical. For "Memorandum Opinions," a parenthetical so indicating ("mem. op.") may be included after the court parenthetical or, if applicable, the per curiam parenthetical:

Richardson v. Kays, No. 02-03-241-CV, 2003 WL 22457054, at *1 (Tex. App.—Fort Worth Oct. 30, 2003, no pet.) (per curiam) (mem. op.).

In re Int'l Profit Assocs., Inc., 274 S.W.3d 696, 697 (Tex. App.—Corpus Christi 2008, orig. proceeding) (per curiam) (mem. op.), *mand. granted*, 274 S.W.3d 672, 680 (Tex. 2009) (per curiam).

(b) Criminal Cases. The courts of appeals must hand down a written opinion in every criminal case. Besides designating the opinion an "Opinion" or a "Memorandum Opinion," every opinion issued in a criminal case by a court of appeals will also bear the notation "publish" or "do not publish." If the case has been designated "do not publish," include a parenthetical ("not designated for publication") following the court parenthetical or, if applicable, the per curiam parenthetical:

Vincent v. State, No. 05-10-00320-CR, 2011 WL 635259, at *1 (Tex. App.—Dallas Feb. 23, 2011, pet. ref'd) (not designated for publication).

State v. Mata, No. 13-97-608-CR, 1998 WL 35276363, at *1 (Tex. App.—Corpus Christi March 12, 1998, no pet.) (per curiam) (not designated for publication).

If the case has been designated both a "Memorandum Opinion" and "do not publish," then place both designations in the same parenthetical, separated by a comma:

State v. Wise, No. 04-04-00695-CR, 2005 WL 2952357, at *1 (Tex. App.—San Antonio Oct. 26, 2005, no pet.) (mem. op., not designated for publication).

Green v. State, No. 12-12-00249-CR, 2012 WL 3116252, at *1 (Tex. App.—Tyler July 31, 2012, no pet.) (per curiam) (mem. op., not designated for publication).

(c) **Pre-2003 Civil Cases.** Prior to January 1, 2003, civil cases could be designated "do not publish." Opinions not designated for publication by the courts of appeals under current or prior rules have no precedential value but may be cited with the notation "not designated for publication" following the court parenthetical or, if applicable, the per curiam parenthetical:

In re Visa USA, No. 05-01-01988-CV, 2002 WL 15928, at *1 (Tex. App.—Dallas 2002, no pet.) (mem. op., not designated for publication).

4.1.3 Recent Decisions—Slip Opinions and Electronic Citations

Citation to recent opinions must be to an electronic medium if possible. Such citations must include the case name; the cause number; a citation to LEXIS or Westlaw if using one of these services (see *The Bluebook* Rule 10.8 on citations to electronic sources); the specific page containing the cited material; a parenthetical, including the name of the court ("Tex. App."), an em dash followed by the city in which that court is located (**Rule 4.3**), the exact date, the writ history or petition history (**Rules 4.4** and **4.5**), and a notation of interlocutory orders, if appropriate (**Rule 4.7**); and parenthetical information regarding the weight of authority, if appropriate (**Rule 4.1.2**):

Baggs v. Becker, No. 03-07-00731-CV, 2009 WL 280664, at *1 (Tex. App.—Austin Feb. 6, 2009, no pet.) (mem. op.).

(a) **Citation to Unpaginated Opinion on Court Website.** Each court of appeals provides recent opinions on the website for that specific court. When citing to an opinion provided on a court's website, a designation of "*available at*" followed by the URL must be provided after the court parenthetical or, if applicable, the parenthetical information regarding the weight of authority.

When citing to a slip opinion provided in a form that does not indicate pagination, use a pinpoint citation to a paragraph or other segment that will best direct the reader to the material cited. Include the designation "slip op." before the paragraph number:

Jaxson v. Morgan, No. 14-04-00785-CV, slip op. ¶ 4 (Tex. App.—Houston [14th Dist.] Apr. 6, 2006, no pet.) (mem. op.), *available at* http://www.search.txcourts.gov/RetrieveDocument.aspx?DocId=1950&Index=***coa14%5cOpinion.

(b) Citation to Paginated Opinion on Court Website. If citing to a paginated version of an opinion on the court's website, follow the citation rules provided in **Rule 4.1.3(a)** but include the page number after the "slip op." designation:

Jenkins v. State, No. 03-13-0632-CR, slip op. at 2 (Tex. App.—Austin Oct. 25, 2013, no pet. h.) (mem. op., not designated for publication), *available at* http://www.search.txcourts.gov/SearchMedia.aspx?MediaVersionID=9a9e6403-aac0-45ac-8e31-27c4d2fd8a33&MediaID=a0ea946d-bccf-4336-9228-581bd0b046c5&coa=%22%20+%20this.CurrentWebState.CurrentCourt%20+%20@%22&DT=Opinion.

(c) Citing to a Case Generally. When citing a case generally, there is no need to include a "slip op." designation:

See generally Jaxson v. Morgan, No. 14-04-00785-CV (Tex App.—Houston [14th Dist.] Apr. 6, 2006, no pet.) (mem. op.), *available at* http://www.search.txcourts.gov/RetrieveDocument.aspx?DocId=1950&Index=***coa14%5cOpinion.

4.2 Courts of Civil Appeals—1892 to 1981

Between 1892 and August 31, 1981, Texas intermediate appellate courts did not have criminal jurisdiction and were known as courts of civil appeals.

4.2.1 Basic Citation Form—1911 to 1981

Prior to the fourteenth edition of *The Greenbook*, cases decided by the courts of civil appeals between 1911 and 1981 were cited as "Tex. Civ. App."—not "Tex. App." in the parenthetical. But the fourteenth edition of *The Greenbook* eliminated this distinction. The "Civ." is no longer needed in the court and date parenthetical of any citation.

Bd. of Adjustment v. Rich, 328 S.W.2d 798 (Tex. App.—Fort Worth 1959, writ ref'd).

4.2.2 Citing to the *Texas Civil Appeals Reports*—1892 to 1911

From 1892 to 1911, the State of Texas published an official reporter containing the decisions of the courts of civil appeals, called the *Texas Civil Appeals Reports* ("Tex. Civ. App."). These cases were also published in the *South Western Reporter*.

Parallel citations to both reporters are not generally required in either legal memoranda or court documents. If, however, a court's local rule requires a parallel citation, citations should include the case name; a citation to the volume and page of the official *Texas Civil Appeals Reports*; the specific page of the *Texas Civil Appeals Reports* containing the cited material; a parallel citation to the *South Western Reporter*; a parenthetical, including the city in which the court is located (**Rule 4.3**), the date, the writ history (**Rule 4.4.2**), and a notation of interlocutory orders, if appropriate (**Rule 4.7**) (the court designation ("Tex. App.") is omitted as redundant); and parenthetical information regarding the weight of authority (**Rule 4.1.2**), if applicable:

Jackson v. Maddox, 53 Tex. Civ. App. 478, 479, 117 S.W. 185, 185 (Fort Worth 1909, no writ).

Jackson, 53 Tex. Civ. App. at 479, 117 S.W. at 185.

4.2.3 Special Citation Format—1876 to 1892

See **Appendix B** for information on citing to decisions from the Texas Court of Appeals between 1876 and 1892.

4.3 Cities

4.3.1 General Rules

A complete citation to any of the first fourteen courts of appeals must include a reference to the city in which the particular court sits. The cities in which these courts of appeals are located are (by district number):

1. Houston [1st Dist.] (formerly Galveston)
2. Fort Worth
3. Austin
4. San Antonio
5. Dallas
6. Texarkana
7. Amarillo
8. El Paso
9. Beaumont
10. Waco
11. Eastland
12. Tyler
13. Corpus Christi–Edinburg
14. Houston [14th Dist.]

In the parenthetical of such a court of appeals citation, the city is *never* abbreviated, contrary to *The Bluebook* Table T10.1.

Note especially that "Fort Worth" is not abbreviated. Note as well that Corpus Christi–Edinburg is connected with an en dash, not a hyphen.

4.3.2 The Houston and Galveston Courts of Appeals

Citation to decisions of the Houston courts of appeals after the creation of the Fourteenth District in 1967 must include a bracketed reference to the district number. Citations to opinions from the old Galveston Court of Civil Appeals should include "Galveston" in the parenthetical:

Abella v. Knight Oil Tools, 945 S.W.2d 847, 849 (Tex. App.—Houston [1st Dist.] 1997, no writ).

Hoppes v. Williams, 213 S.W. 328, 329 (Tex. App.—Galveston 1919, no writ).

4.3.3 The Fifteenth Court of Appeals

Citation to decisions of the Fifteenth Court of Appeals do not include a reference to the city in which the court sits. This distinction reflects the Fifteenth Court of Appeals' unique, statewide appellate jurisdiction over a limited range of legal matters.

In re Google, 705 S.W.3d 479, 484 (Tex. App.—15th Dist. 2025, no pet. h.).

4.3.4 *South Western Reporter* — Cases Before 1912

Before 1912, the *South Western Reporter* did not provide the city (district) in which the particular court of civil appeals that decided the case was located. To determine the city for citation, consult **Appendix J** and match the last name of the judge with the appropriate city.

4.4 Civil Cases — Petition and Writ History

Unless a subsequent history designation is appropriate under **Rule 4.6**, a complete citation for civil cases in a court of appeals *must* include a notation showing the Texas Supreme Court's disposition of the particular case.

Petition History. For cases in which the petition was filed on or after September 1, 1997, provide the petition history per **Rule 4.4.1**.

Writ History. For cases in which the writ was filed before September 1, 1997, provide the writ history per **Rule 4.4.2**.

Petition/Writ History as Subsequent History. Where the Texas Supreme Court or the Court of Criminal Appeals publishes an opinion explaining its reasoning in acting on a petition for review, such a decision *must* be cited as subsequent history per **Rule 4.6.1(b)**.

▸ Practice Tip

Locating Petition & Writ History Information

West's *Texas Subsequent History Table* was a cumulative list of the petition and writ history of every published Texas case. It was discontinued after October 2014. If your case predates October 2012 and you have access to the final edition or a law library carrying one, we suggest looking there. For more recent cases, check the commercial databases discussed below or review a court's weekly orders on the Texas Judicial Branch's website at www.txcourts.gov.

Petition status and history is often available electronically through LEXIS or Westlaw. On Westlaw, the subsequent history can be accessed by clicking on the "History" link for the case. (Note that Westlaw uses the phrase "review denied" instead of "petition for review denied.") On LEXIS, this information is available at the top of the opinion by clicking "History" or in the "*Shepard's*®" panel on the right side of the opinion.

The Texas Judicial Branch provides information on petition and writ dispositions on its website, www.search.txcourts.gov. This information can be located by searching for the case number in the relevant court.

Recent filings of petition applications and recent petition dispositions can also be found in the advance sheets of the *Texas Supreme Court Journal*, but they are not cumulative.

4.4.1 Petition History (On or After September 1, 1997)

Use these forms of citation to describe the status of a petition for review:

1. no pet. h.
2. no pet.
3. pet. filed
4. pet. dism'd by agr.
5. pet. withdrawn
6. pet. dism'd w.o.j.
7. pet. denied
8. pet. ref'd
9. pet. struck
10. pet. dism'd
11. pet. granted, judgm't vacated w.r.m.
12. pet. granted
13. pet. abated
14. pet. pending

For an explanation and table of the appropriate abbreviations (and relevant caveats) for notations on petition history, see **Appendix D**.

▸ **Practice Tip**

When to use "no pet. h." versus "no pet."

If no motion for rehearing is timely filed with the appeals court, parties have 45 days after the entry of judgment to file a petition with the Texas Supreme Court. If a motion for rehearing is timely filed, parties have 45 days after the appeals court's last ruling to file a petition with the Texas Supreme Court.

The "no pet. h." designation is used when the time for filing a petition for review with the Texas Supreme Court has not yet passed. The "no pet." designation is used when the deadline for filing a petition for review has passed and none was filed.

4.4.2 Writ History (Before September 1, 1997)

Use the following forms of citation to describe the status of an application for writ of error:

1. no writ
2. writ dism'd by agr.
3. writ dism'd
4. writ dism'd w.o.j.
5. writ dism'd judgm't
6. writ ref'd w.o.m.
7. writ ref'd n.r.e.
8. writ denied
9. writ ref'd
10. writ granted w.r.m. cor.
11. writ granted

For an explanation and table of the appropriate abbreviations (and relevant caveats) for notations on writ history see **Appendix E**.

4.5 Criminal Cases—Petition History

Unless a subsequent history designation is appropriate under **Rule 4.6**, a complete citation for intermediate criminal cases *must* include the history of the petition for review indicating how the Texas Court of Criminal Appeals has disposed of the case cited.

Petition History as Subsequent History. Where the Court of Criminal Appeals publishes an opinion explaining its reasons for dismissing a petition as improvidently granted or for otherwise refusing a petition for review, the opinion should be cited as subsequent history per **Rule 4.6.1(b)**.

▸ Practice Tip

Locating Petition History Information

West's *Texas Subsequent History Table* was a cumulative list of the petition and writ history of every published Texas case. It was discontinued after October 2014. If your case predates October 2012 and you have access to the final edition or a law library carrying one, we suggest looking there. For more recent cases, check the commercial databases discussed below or review a court's weekly orders on the Texas Judicial Branch's website at www.txcourts.gov.

Petition status and history is often available electronically through LEXIS or Westlaw. On Westlaw, the subsequent history can be accessed by clicking on the "History" link for the case. (Note that Westlaw uses the phrase "review denied" instead of "petition for review denied.") On LEXIS, this information is available at the top of the opinion by clicking "History" or in the "*Shepard's*®" panel on the right side of the opinion.

The Texas Judicial Branch provides information on petition and writ dispositions on its website, www.search.txcourts.gov. This information can be located by searching for the case number in the relevant court.

Use the following designations:

1. no pet. h.
2. no pet.
3. pet. filed
4. pet. dism'd
5. pet. ref'd, untimely filed
6. pet. ref'd
7. pet. granted
8. rev. granted, without pet.

▸ Practice Tip

When to use "no pet. h." versus "no pet."

A criminal defendant generally has 30 days after the day judgment was entered by the court of appeals, or the day the last timely motion for rehearing was overruled, in which to petition the Texas Court of Criminal Appeals for review.

The "no pet. h." designation is used when the time for filing a petition for review with the Texas Court of Criminal Appeals has not yet passed. The "no pet." designation is used when the deadline for filing a petition for review has passed and none was filed.

For an explanation and table of the appropriate abbreviations (and relevant caveats) for notations on petition history for the Court of Criminal Appeals see **Appendix F**.

4.5.1 Writs of Habeas Corpus and Prohibition

When citing a case in which an application for either a writ of habeas corpus or a writ of prohibition has been made, the citation will refer to the subsequent disposition only if the disposition is relevant to the proposition for which the case is cited. Cite the subsequent disposition according to **Rule 4.6**:

Massoth v. State, No. 14-03-00605-CR, 2004 WL 1381027, at *1 (Tex. App.—Houston [14th Dist.] June 22, 2004, pet. ref'd) (mem. op., not designated for publication), *habeas corpus granted in part sub nom. Ex parte Massoth*, No. AP-75215, 2005 WL 1774115, at *1 (Tex. Crim. App. July 27, 2005) (per curiam) (not designated for publication).

4.6 Subsequent History

4.6.1 Subsequent History—State Courts

(a) General Rule. The subsequent history of a court of appeals case is given for *any* disposition by the Texas Supreme Court after granting a petition or writ, or by the Texas Court of Criminal Appeals after granting a petition (or after review on its own motion). See *The Bluebook* Rule 10.7 and Table T8 for a partial list of phrases used in describing subsequent histories.

The year of the lower court's decision should appear only if it differs from the year of the higher court's decision:

RepublicBank Dallas, N.A. v. Interkal, Inc., 677 S.W.2d 759, 762 (Tex. App.—Dallas 1984), *rev'd on other grounds*, 691 S.W.2d 605, 607 (Tex. 1985).

Brinegar v. Porterfield, 705 S.W.2d 236, 241 (Tex. App.—Texarkana), *aff'd*, 719 S.W.2d 558, 560 (Tex. 1986).

(b) Petition/Writ History as Subsequent History. When either the Texas Supreme Court or Court of Criminal Appeals has given a reason for granting or refusing a request for review, include that information as subsequent history rather than designating it as petition or writ history.

The year of the lower court's decision ought to appear only if it differs from the year of the higher court's decision:

Cockerham v. State, 703 S.W.2d 334 (Tex. App.—Corpus Christi 1985), *pet. dism'd, improvidently granted*, 729 S.W.2d 742 (Tex. Crim. App. 1987).

Weaver v. Westchester Fire Ins. Co., 730 S.W.2d 834 (Tex. App.—Waco), *writ ref'd*, 739 S.W.2d 23 (Tex. 1987) (per curiam).

4.6.2 Subsequent History—Supreme Court of the United States

A disposition by the Supreme Court of the United States is given in addition to writ or petition history.

The year of the lower court's decision ought to appear only if it differs from the year of the higher court's decision:

In re Baby Girl S., 628 S.W.2d 261, 262 (Tex. App.—Eastland 1982, writ ref'd n.r.e.), *vacated sub nom. Kirkpatrick v. Christian Homes, Inc.*, 460 U.S. 1074, 1075 (1983).

4.6.3 Other Subsequent History

Omit the history of a case on remand, any denial of rehearing, and, in a case over two years old, any denial of certiorari, unless the subsequent history is relevant to the point for which the case is cited.

4.7 Interlocutory Orders

4.7.1 Basic Citation Form

A citation to a civil case in which the court of appeals publishes an opinion in support of an order follows **Rule 4.1** or **Rule 4.2**, as appropriate, but must include the notation "order" within the parenthetical, immediately following the year:

Sheerin v. Exxon Corp., 923 S.W.2d 52 (Tex. App.—Houston [1st Dist.] 1995, order).

4.7.2 Subsequent Opinion on the Merits

If the court of appeals publishes an opinion on the merits after final judgment in the same case as the order cited, then the opinion on the merits *must* be included as subsequent history:

Coronado v. State, 996 S.W.2d 283, 285 (Tex. App.—Waco 1999, order) (per curiam), *disp. on merits*, 25 S.W.3d 806, 811 (Tex. App.—Waco 2000, pet. ref'd).

Burrhus v. M & S Mach. & Supply Co., 897 S.W.2d 871, 872 (Tex. App.—San Antonio 1995, order), *disp. on merits sub nom. Burrhus v. M&S Supply, Inc.*, 933 S.W.2d 635, 637 (Tex. App.—San Antonio 1996, writ denied).

5 Commission of Appeals

At three separate points in its history, Texas established appellate commissions to alleviate the workload of its high courts. The first two periods are covered immediately below. See **Appendix C** for information on the Texas Commission of Appeals, operating from 1879–1892. Information regarding a court's treatment of a Commission decision is available in the *South Western Reporter*, LEXIS, and Westlaw, immediately following the Commission opinion.

5.1 Commission in Aid of the Court of Criminal Appeals—1925 to Date

Historical Note

Commissioners have been appointed at various times since 1925 by the governor or the Texas Court of Criminal Appeals. Article V, § 4 of the Texas Constitution provides continuing authority for the Texas Court of Criminal Appeals to appoint commissioners, although this authority has not been exercised recently.

When an opinion issued by commissioners has been approved by a majority of the Court of Criminal Appeals, cite it as if it were an opinion of that court per **Rule 3.1** or **Rule 3.2**.

Pinkston v. State, 69 S.W.2d 60, 61 (1934).

5.2 Texas Commission of Appeals of the Texas Supreme Court—1918 to 1945

When citing cases decided by the Commission of Appeals of the Texas Supreme Court (1918–1945), it is important to determine whether the Texas Supreme Court adopted or approved the Commission's entire opinion or whether it merely adopted the Commission's judgment or approved the holding. The Texas Supreme Court discussed the precedential value of these various possible dispositions in *National Bank of Commerce v. Williams*, 84 S.W.2d 691, 692 (Tex. 1935).

The Texas Supreme Court adopted every Commission opinion issued on or after March 21, 1934, so always cite those decisions in accordance with **Rule 5.2.2**.

5.2.1 Judgment Rendered, No Further Action Taken

The Texas Supreme Court may render the judgment recommended by the Commission without any indication of other action taken. These "unadopted" or "unapproved" opinions are not binding to the same extent as other Commission opinions. When citing to these opinions, include a parenthetical indicating the court designation ("Tex. Comm'n App.") and the year of decision:

Express Publ'g Co. v. Keeran, 284 S.W. 913, 914 (Tex. Comm'n App. 1926).

5.2.2 Opinion Adopted or Approved

If the Texas Supreme Court adopted or approved the entire opinion of the Commission, then the opinion has the full authority of a Texas Supreme Court decision. To indicate that the opinion was not written by the Texas Supreme Court, while showing the appropriate precedential value, cite the case as though it were a decision of the Texas Supreme Court per **Rule 2.1.1**, with the addition of "Comm'n Op." in brackets after "Tex.":

Cheney v. Coffey, 114 S.W.2d 533, 534 (Tex. [Comm'n Op.] 1938).

5.2.3 Holding Approved

Where the Texas Supreme Court has approved the holding of a Commission decision, it signifies that the court adopted the judgment and approved the specific holding of the Commission discussed in the opinion but did not necessarily approve its reasoning. Cite such cases per **Rule 5.2.1**, with the notation "holding approved" following the year of decision in the parenthetical:

Gueringer v. St. Louis, B. & M. Ry., 23 S.W.2d 704, 706 (Tex. Comm'n App. 1930, holding approved).

5.2.4 Judgment Adopted, Affirmed, or Approved

Where the Texas Supreme Court adopts, affirms, or approves the judgment of a Commission decision, this indicates that the court approved neither the Commission's opinion, nor its holding, nor its reasoning on any particular point.[1] The Texas Supreme Court has merely rendered the judgment recommended by the Commission and has adopted, affirmed, or approved the judgment. Cite such cases per **Rule 5.2.1**, with the appropriate notation "judgm't adopted," "judgm't approved," or "judgm't affirmed" following the year of decision in the parenthetical. If the Court explicitly approves the holding and adopts, approves, or affirms the judgment, include both notations within the same parenthetical:

Prairie Oil & Gas Co. v. State, 231 S.W. 1088, 1091 (Tex. Comm'n App. 1921, judgm't adopted).

Humble Oil & Ref. Co. v. Davis, 296 S.W. 285, 288 (Tex. Comm'n App. 1927, judgm't affirmed).

McKenzie v. Withers, 206 S.W. 503, 505 (Tex. Comm'n App. 1918, judgm't approved).

Young v. Blain, 245 S.W. 65, 66 (Tex. Comm'n App. 1922, holding approved, judgm't adopted).

1. "[O]ur approval of the judgment recommended by the Commission is to be understood as having no further effect than to simply adopt the view of the Commission as the determination to be made of the cause." *McKenzie v. Withers*, 206 S.W. 503, 503 (Tex. 1918). "It is not to be construed as an approval by the Supreme Court of the opinion of the Commission in the particular case, or the reasons given in the Commission's opinion for its conclusion." *Id.*

6 Mandamus and Other Original Proceedings

► **Practice Tip**

Original proceedings can be brought in appellate courts to obtain extraordinary relief and include such remedies as a writ of habeas corpus, mandamus, prohibition, and injunction. If a court denies relief in an original proceeding, it may issue an opinion but does not have to do so. The court must issue an opinion when it grants relief in an original proceeding. For complete rules on original proceedings in appellate courts see Rule 52 of the Texas Rules of Appellate Procedure.

6.1 Original Proceedings in the Texas Supreme Court

Cite mandamus cases and other original proceedings in the Texas Supreme Court like other Texas Supreme Court cases (see **Chapter 2**). Include the designation "orig. proceeding" in a separate parenthetical following the date parenthetical:

Flores v. Fourth Court of Appeals, 777 S.W.2d 38, 39 (Tex. 1989) (orig. proceeding).

6.2 Mandamus in the Courts of Appeals

When citing mandamus proceedings in the courts of appeals, citations should follow the rules in **Chapter 4**, but indicate the nature of the proceeding in the parenthetical rather than writ or petition history.

6.2.1 No Action Taken by the Texas Supreme Court

For original proceedings in the courts of appeals in which the Texas Supreme Court has taken no action, replace the writ or petition history with the designation "orig. proceeding" following the year of decision in the parenthetical:

In re Ruiz, 16 S.W.3d 921, 923 (Tex. App.—Waco 2000, orig. proceeding).

Owens v. Wallace, 821 S.W.2d 746, 747 (Tex. App.—Tyler 1992, orig. proceeding).

6.2.2 Mandamus Pending in the Texas Supreme Court

If a petition for a writ of mandamus is pending in the Texas Supreme Court, include the designation "mand. pending" in brackets within the date parenthetical:

In re Luna, No. 01-03-01055-CV, 2004 WL 2005935, at *1 (Tex. App.—Houston [1st Dist.] Sept. 9, 2004, orig. proceeding [mand. pending]).

6.2.3 Overriding Writs from the Texas Supreme Court

When the Texas Supreme Court issues a writ of mandamus overriding an order by a court of appeals, cite the Supreme Court case as subsequent history according to **Rule 4.6**. Include the designation *"mand. granted"* before the Supreme Court citation:

Contico Int'l, Inc. v. Alvarez, 910 S.W.2d 29, 32 (Tex. App.—El Paso 1995, orig. proceeding), *mand. granted sub nom. Mendoza v. Eighth Court of Appeals*, 917 S.W.2d 787, 789 (Tex. 1996) (per curiam).

6.2.4 Denial of Mandamus Relief by the Texas Supreme Court—On or After September 1, 1997

(a) Denial Without Opinion. If the Texas Supreme Court denies mandamus relief without issuing an opinion, include the designation "mand. denied" in brackets within the date parenthetical:

In re Onstad, 20 S.W.3d 731, 733 (Tex. App.—Texarkana 2000, orig. proceeding [mand. denied]).

(b) **Denial Accompanied by an Opinion.** If the Texas Supreme Court issues an opinion denying mandamus relief, cite the Supreme Court case as subsequent history according to **Rule 4.6**. Include the designation "*mand. denied*" before the Supreme Court citation:

In re Tex. Farmers Ins. Exch., 990 S.W.2d 337, 343 (Tex. App.—Texarkana 1999, orig. proceeding), *mand. denied*, 12 S.W.3d 807, 808 (Tex. 2000).

6.2.5 Denial of Mandamus Relief by the Texas Supreme Court—Before September 1, 1997

Before September 1, 1997, the Texas Rules of Appellate Procedure required a petition for mandamus to be accompanied by a motion for leave to file.

(a) **Denial of Leave.** When citing a petition for a writ of mandamus in an intermediate court, include the designation "leave denied" in brackets if the Texas Supreme Court denied leave to file a petition for mandamus for the same underlying cause:

May v. Lawrence, 751 S.W.2d 678, 679 (Tex. App.—Tyler 1988, orig. proceeding [leave denied]) (per curiam).

(b) **Grant of Leave Followed by Denial of Relief.** If the Texas Supreme Court granted a motion for leave to file a writ of mandamus, but eventually *denied* mandamus relief, cite the opinion of the court of appeals according to **Rule 6.2.1**. Cite the Texas Supreme Court case as subsequent history according to **Rule 4.6**. Include the designation "*leave granted, mand. denied*" before the Texas Supreme Court citation:

Gen. Motors Corp. v. Gayle, 924 S.W.2d 222, 224 (Tex. App.—Houston [14th Dist.] 1996, orig. proceeding), *leave granted, mand. denied*, 940 S.W.2d 598, 599 (Tex. 1997) (per curiam).

7 Trial Courts

▸ Practice Tip

The Texas court structure contains three levels of trial courts: local trial courts of limited jurisdiction, county trial courts of limited jurisdiction, and state trial courts of general and special jurisdiction.

The local-level courts consist of Justice Courts, which are created by the Texas Constitution, and Municipal Courts, which are created by the Texas Legislature. Both courts have limited jurisdiction over minor civil and criminal matters, and Municipal Courts have exclusive jurisdiction over the enforcement of city ordinances.

The county-level courts consist of Constitutional County Courts, County Courts at Law, and Statutory Probate Courts. The Texas Constitution requires one Constitutional County Court per county to oversee matters including minor civil, criminal, juvenile, and probate proceedings, as well as appeals from the local-level courts. To relieve the caseload of the Constitutional County Courts of larger counties, the Legislature has created the Statutory Probate Courts, which have original and exclusive jurisdiction over probate matters in the counties where they exist, and the County Courts at Law, which generally have concurrent jurisdiction, although jurisdiction varies under the statutes creating these courts.

Finally, the District Courts are the only statutory trial courts of general and special jurisdiction over civil, criminal, juvenile, or family law matters.

7.1 Basic Citation Form

Citation of Texas district and trial court cases must include the case name, the cause number, and a parenthetical indicating the court and the exact date. For district courts, also include the name of the county in which the court sits:

State v. Auguillard, No. 139002101010 (338th Dist. Ct., Harris Cnty, Tex. Oct. 21, 2013).

Batra v. Waggoner, No. 002-02559-2012 (Collin Cnty. Ct. at Law No. 2, Tex. Oct. 21, 2013).

Lipset v. McNertray, No. 011-93356-05 (Bexar Cnty. Prob. Ct. No. 2, Tex. Sept. 29, 1985).

7.1.1 Citation of Business Court Cases

Cite all reported Business Court cases to the Business Court public domain cite and to the South Western Reporter, if available. A complete citation must contain the case name; the Business Court public domain cite; the specific paragraph containing the cited material; a citation to the volume and page of the South Western Reporter; the specific page containing the cited material; and a parenthetical including the division number and year:

Lone Star NGL Prod. Services LLC v. EagleClaw Midstream Ventures, LLC, 2024 Tex. Bus. 8, ¶ 2, 705 S.W.3d 243, 246 (11th Div. 2024).

Citations to unreported Business Court cases and cases not yet appearing in the South Western Reporter advance sheets should follow this form:

Sebastian v. Durant, 2025 Tex. Bus. 4, ¶ 10, 2025 WL 394634, at *2 (11th Div. 2025).

7.2 Court Abbreviations

Abbreviate court names in accordance with *The Bluebook* Table T7.

Smith Const. Cnty. Ct.

Collin Cnty. Ct. at Law No. 2.

Bexar Cnty. Prob. Ct. No. 2.

7.3 Citations to the Record on Appeal

When citing trial court opinions in briefs to appellate courts, use parenthetical references to the record on appeal. Both the cause number and style from the lower court are omitted from the parenthetical.

The volume number for the record may be given as a Roman numeral or an Arabic numeral. Match the citation format to the numeral type used by the court.

For further guidance on formatting citations to the record on appeal see *The Bluebook* Bluepages B17.

7.3.1 Record on Appeal—On or After September 1, 1997

If support for the textual proposition appears in the reporter's record in the record on appeal, use the abbreviation "R.R.":

Smith began working on March 7, 1990, and remained there until he resigned in December 1994 (II R.R. at 16, XXIX R.R. at 12).

If the textual proposition is supported in the clerk's record, use the abbreviation "C.R.":

Alverson asserted several affirmative defenses (I C.R. at 9, 12–13).

When citing to a supplemental clerk's record, use the abbreviation "Suppl.":

The court subsequently issued findings of fact regarding the special appearance (I Suppl. at 3).

7.3.2 Record on Appeal—Before September 1, 1997

For records created before September 1, 1997, the reporter's record should be cited as "S.F." (statement of facts) and the clerk's record should be cited as "Tr." (transcript).

7.3.3 Exhibits

When citing an exhibit, indicate which party offered the exhibit. To prevent confusion, a shortened form of a particular party's name may be used if there are multiple parties and exhibits:

Smith signed the contract (Pl.'s Ex. 4).

George forged the signature (Smith Ex. 7, Jones Ex. 22, C.R. at 27).

7.4 Court Filings

When citing briefs, motions, or memoranda, follow the conventions in *The Bluebook* Rule 10.8.3.

8 Judicial Misconduct Tribunals

8.1 Special Court of Review

The Texas Special Court of Review, created in 1987, consists of a three-judge panel of courts of appeals justices. The Chief Justice of the Texas Supreme Court selects these justices by lot. The court conducts de novo reviews of sanctions issued by the State Commission on Judicial Conduct. The decisions of the court are not appealable. A citation should include the case name; a citation to the volume and page of the *South Western Reporter*; the specific page containing the cited material; and a parenthetical, including the name of the court ("Tex. Spec. Ct. Rev.") and the year of decision:

In re Sheppard, 815 S.W.2d 917, 918 (Tex. Spec. Ct. Rev. 1991).

8.2 Review Tribunal

The Texas Review Tribunal, created in 1987, consists of a seven-judge panel of justices from the courts of appeals. The Chief Justice of the Texas Supreme Court selects these justices by lot. The tribunal reviews recommendations by the State Commission on Judicial Conduct for the removal or forced retirement of a judge. The decisions of the tribunal are appealable to the Texas Supreme Court. A citation should include the case name; a citation to the volume and page of the *South Western Reporter*; the specific page containing the cited material; and a parenthetical, including the name of the court ("Tex. Rev. Trib."), the year of decision, and any subsequent history or appeal history ("no appeal" or "appeal filed"):

In re Thoma, 873 S.W.2d 477, 491 (Tex. Rev. Trib. 1994, no appeal).

PART III
CONSTITUTIONAL DOCUMENTS

9 Texas Constitution

9.1 Current Constitution

Abbreviate the current Texas constitution, adopted in 1876, as "Tex. Const." Indicate articles using Roman numerals and sections using Arabic numerals. When citing a constitutional provision currently in force, do not include a date:

Tex. Const. art. III, § 5(a).

For prior constitutions of the State of Texas, the State of Coahuila and Texas Constitution, and the Republic of Texas Constitution see **Appendix G**.

9.1.1 Short Form

Constitutional provisions may be cited using "*id.*" where "*id.*" would otherwise be appropriate. Where "*id.*" is inappropriate, the full citation is repeated. For further explanation, see *The Bluebook* Rule 11.

9.2 Repealed, Amended, and Expired Provisions

When citing a provision of the Texas constitution that has since been repealed or amended, or citing a provision that has an expiration date, indicate parenthetically the action taken—repeal ("repealed"), amendment ("amended"), or expiration ("expired" or "expires")—and the date of that action. Include an exact date if relevant, otherwise give only the year. In the case of amendment, include only the most recent amendment date:

Tex. Const. art. V, § 6 (amended 2001).

Tex. Const. art. XVI, § 70 (expired Sept. 1, 2008).

Tex. Const. art. XII, § 6 (repealed Nov. 2, 1993).

9.3 Temporary or Transitional Provisions

Some amendments to the Texas constitution come with temporary or transitional provisions. Cite such provisions to the joint resolution proposing the amendment (**Rule 14.1.2**).

Indicate parenthetically the exact date on which the temporary provision expires or expired:

Tex. Const. temp. provision (a), Tex. H.R.J. Res. 58, § 3, 76th Leg., R.S., 1999 Tex. Gen. Laws 6610, 6611 (expires Jan. 1, 2030).

Tex. Const. temp. provision (b), Tex. S.J. Res. 1, § 1, 74th Leg., R.S., 1995 Tex. Gen. Laws 6427, 6427 (expired Sept. 1, 1997).

9.4 Interpretive Commentaries

Interpretive commentaries follow many provisions of the current constitution in *Vernon's Annotated Constitution of the State of Texas*. Cite these commentaries by the longest full subdivision of the constitution to which the commentary applies, followed by "interp. commentary" and a parenthetical notation of the name of the publisher ("West") and the date of publication of the cited volume:

Tex. Const. art. VIII, § 1 interp. commentary (West 2007).

PART IV

TEXAS STATUTES

10 Current Statutes

Format Guide

Current Statutes in Subject Matter Codes	Tex. Tax Code Ann. § 26.06(a).
Current Uncodified Statutes	Tex. Rev. Civ. Stat. Ann. art. 581-4(A).
Session Laws	Act of May 27, 2005, 79th Leg., R.S., ch. 484, § 2, sec. 153.433, 2005 Tex. Gen. Laws 1345.
Statutes Cited to Electronic Database	Tex. Alco. Bev. Code Ann. § 251.71(a).

▸ Practice Guide

Subject Matter Codes

The 1925 Revised Statutes was a complete reenactment of Texas law, arranged alphabetically by subject and numbered sequentially by article. Laws enacted after 1925 that did not amend the Revised Statutes were arranged unofficially and assigned an article number by Thompson West. In 1963, the Texas Legislature passed a statute creating the continuing statutory revision program. The project envisioned twenty-seven codes organized on a decimal system. All twenty-seven codes have now been enacted at least partially. On January 1, 2014, the last of the wholly unenacted codes, the Estates Code, took effect and should now be cited instead of the old Probate Code.

The project continues, however, and the following considerations should be kept in mind. Because of its large volume, the Special District Local Laws Code has been enacted in parts and continues to be under revision. Additionally, Title 1 of the Insurance Code contains the unrevised 1959 Insurance Code, although it should be cited as part of the current Insurance Code. Finally, although Title 2 of the Code of Criminal Procedure was added as part of the revision program, it must continue to be cited as part of the old code until the as-yet unenacted Criminal Procedure Code takes effect. For more complete guidance on citing the Insurance Code and the Code of Criminal Procedure, see **Rule 10.2.2(a)** and **Rule 10.2.2(d)**. The Texas Legislative Council publishes up-to-date information on the codification project, both on its website and in its *Drafting Manual* (available on its website).

Cite all current statutes to the new subject matter codes (**Rule 10.2.1** and **Appendix H**) if they appear there. Otherwise, cite *Vernon's Annotated Revised Civil Statutes of the State of Texas* or one of the independent codes (**Rule 10.2.4**).

10.1 Generally Applicable Rules

Historical Note

West Publishing & Vernon Law Book Co.

Vernon Law Book Co. was the publisher of the original 1925 Revised Statutes, known as *Vernon's Annotated Revised Civil Statutes of the State of Texas*. This is still the title of the book that contains the current uncodified statutes.

Although West Publishing (now Thompson West) purchased Vernon Law Book Co. in 1969, prior editions of *The Greenbook* required citations to "Vernon" as the publisher in the parenthetical following the statute or code.

The twelfth edition changed this convention to indicate the actual publisher in the parenthetical ("West").

The fourteenth edition eliminated the publisher and publication year for current and in-force statutes.

10.1.1 Sections and Articles

One potentially confusing element of Texas statute citation is the distinction between sections and articles. The subject matter codes are divided into sections. Uncodified statutes, Title 1 of the new Insurance Code, and independent codes are divided into articles. (For more information on Title 1 of the Insurance Code, see **Rule 10.2.2(a)**.) Compare:

Tex. Ins. Code Ann. § 823.456.

Tex. Ins. Code Ann. art. 5.06.

Tex. Rev. Civ. Stat. Ann. art. 581-4(A).

10.1.2 Citations for Historical Fact

When a statute is cited for the historical fact of its enactment, amendment, or repeal, cite to the session laws according to **Rule 10.3** and **Rule 11.1**.

10.1.3 Pamphlets, Supplements, and Pocket Parts

Cite statutes appearing in pamphlets that supplement bound volumes, or in pocket parts of bound volumes, like other statutes but include the abbreviation "Supp." in a final parenthetical:

Tex. Alco. Bev. Code Ann. § 22.03 (Supp.).

Do not, however, use the abbreviation "Supp." when citing a pamphlet that does not supplement a bound volume. Such pamphlets are used to publish newly enacted codes that have not yet appeared in hardbound volumes (cited according to **Rule 10.2.1**) and auxiliary laws (cited according to **Rule 10.2.5**).

10.1.4 Citation of Multiple Provisions

When citing two or more statutory provisions, use the forms outlined below. The subject matter codes are divided into sections. Uncodified statutes, Title 1 of the Insurance Code, and the independent codes are divided into articles.

(a) Multiple Sections Within the Subject Matter Codes. Cite multiple sections of a subject matter code in numerical order beginning with the lowest section number.

If all cited provisions are current or appear in volumes or supplements bearing the same date, use two section symbols and, if necessary, a single date parenthetical:

Tex. Health & Safety Code Ann. §§ 286.101, 433.045.

(b) Multiple Articles Within the Uncodified Statutes, Title 1 of the Insurance Code, or Within the Same Independent Code. Cite multiple articles within *Vernon's Annotated Revised Civil Statutes of the State of Texas,* Title 1 of the Texas Insurance Code, or the same independent code in numerical order beginning with the lowest article number. Articles are often subdivided into sections; cite multiple sections within an article in numerical order beginning with the lowest section number.

If all cited articles are current and do not include a citation to a section number, use the designation "arts.":

Tex. Rev. Civ. Stats. Ann. arts. 4512.5, 5196b.

A separate "art." or "arts." designation is required for any article that includes a citation to a section number and for the article or group of articles immediately following it:

Tex. Rev. Civ. Stats. Ann. art. 4512.5, art. 5415e-4, § 2(a), arts. 5421b, 5421b-1.

Tex. Rev. Civ. Stats. Ann. art. 6243g-4, art. 6243i, § 1.02(2), art. 6243j, art. 6243n.

10.2 Current Statutes

Before using this section, please consult the **Practice Tip** at the start of **Chapter 10** for an overview of the Texas Codes.

10.2.1 Codified Statutes

Cite material in these statutes to the subject matter codes or, if appropriate, their supplements. The citation must include the name of the subject matter code and the section number. If a statute is currently in force, cite it without indicating the date of publication:

Tex. Tax Code § 26.06(a)(Supp.).

Appendix H includes a table of code title abbreviations and examples of each.

10.2.2 Recent, Incomplete, and Forthcoming Codification

The legislature continues to revise and codify Texas statutes. Begin citing each of the new codes when indicated by its effective date. Special considerations include:

(a) **Insurance Code.** Title 1 includes provisions of the Insurance Code of 1951, as amended, that have not been revised as part of the Council's statutory revision program. It is appropriate to cite articles in Title 1 as part of the "Insurance Code." See **Rules 10.1.1** and **10.1.4(b)** for more information on citing Title 1 of the Insurance Code.

(b) **Business Organizations Code.** As of January 1, 2010, the Business Organizations Code applies to all entities formed or doing business in Texas. For further information about this effective date, consult Chapter 402 of the Business Organizations Code, in particular § 402.005.

(c) **Special District Local Laws Code.** Its codification is ongoing. Ultimately it will encompass all or most local laws that govern individual special districts that were previously not published except within the volumes of legislative session laws. Special district laws not yet included in the subject matter code are cited to the enacting session law according to **Rule 10.3**.

Codified special district laws are cited per **Rule 10.2.1**. Some individual special district laws were previously codified in other subject matter codes, such as the Local Government Code and the Water Code. Unless or until they are moved to the Special District Local Laws Code, they are cited as originally codified.

(d) Criminal Procedure Code. The Legislature has not codified the 1965 Code of Criminal Procedure, but in 1985 it enacted Title 2, Code of Criminal Procedure, which codified miscellaneous criminal procedure statutes omitted from the 1965 code. Until the Code is completely codified, all uncodified provisions are cited to the independent code. The subject matter code is tentatively titled the Criminal Procedure Code and will be cited as follows:

Tex. Crim. Proc. Code Ann. § [*x*].

(e) Estates Code. All material previously in the Probate Code has now been codified as the Estates Code. The Estates Code became effective on January 1, 2014. Before it became effective, West published the Estates Code as a pamphlet accompanying the 2013 Election Code. Cite to this pamphlet version of the Estates Code by indicating as such in a parenthetical. Once West has published a fully annotated version, cite the Estates Code like all other codes per **Rule 10.2.2**. The Estates Code should be abbreviated as "Tex. Est. Code Ann.":

Tex. Est. Code Ann. § 201.001 (pamphlet).

10.2.3 Uncodified Statutes

Most statutes not yet incorporated into the subject matter codes are found in *Vernon's Annotated Revised Civil Statutes of the State of Texas*. These statutes are organized by articles, which are further subdivided into sections. They are cited as follows:

Tex. Rev. Civ. Stat. Ann. art. 5415e-4, § 2(a).

10.2.4 Statutes in the Independent Codes

▸ Practice Tip

Before citing to the independent codes, verify that the article or section is still effective. Citations should not be made to an independent code if a provision has been replaced by a subject matter code. But note that some of the superseded independent codes may still apply if the transaction occurred before the effective date.

Vernon's Annotated Revised Civil Statutes of the State of Texas includes one independent code not yet fully superseded by a subject matter code: the Texas Code of Criminal Procedure. It and the other, superseded independent codes are organized by articles. Cite statutes in the independent codes as follows:

Tex. Code Crim. Pro. Ann. art. 13.25, § (a).

Appendix H contains a table of independent code abbreviations for the current and recently superseded independent codes.

10.2.5 Auxiliary Laws

Some special and local laws that were neither repealed by, nor incorporated into, a new subject matter code are listed (but not reprinted) in auxiliary pamphlets that accompany the code. In most cases, these laws no longer appear in *Vernon's Annotated Revised Civil Statutes of the State of Texas*. Citations to the auxiliary pamphlets therefore include a bracketed session law citation (**Rule 10.3**):

Tex. Educ. Aux. Laws art. 2668b [Act of Mar. 28, 1963, 58th Leg., R.S., ch. 39, 1963 Tex. Gen. Laws 59].

Tex. Water Aux. Laws art. 8280-178 [Act of May 24, 1955, 54th Leg., R.S., ch. 401, 1955 Tex. Gen. Laws 1067].

The Water Auxiliary Laws pamphlet also contains the text of laws considered general and permanent that were not incorporated into the Water Code. These laws are cited to the auxiliary laws pamphlet without including session information:

Tex. Water Aux. Laws art. 7844.

10.3 Session Laws

▸ Practice Tip

Cite a statute to the official session law only in these four circumstances:

If the statute has not yet appeared in one of the codes or *Vernon's Annotated Revised Civil Statutes of the State of Texas*;

If the statute is being cited for the historical fact of its enactment;

If there is a material difference between the statute and the enacting session law and the document references the original version; or

If the statute has subsequently expired or been amended or repealed (see **Rule 11.1**).

The elements of a session law citation are: the name of the statute (**Rule 10.3.1**); the legislature and session of enactment (**Rule 10.3.2**); the chapter and section number of the statute (**Rule 10.3.3**); the publication (**Rule 10.3.4**); and the future location in the code **(Rule 10.3.5)**:

Act of May 30, 2005, 79th Leg., R.S., ch. 268, § 1.06, 2005 Tex. Gen. Laws 621, 623 (codified at Tex. Fam. Code § 107.013(c)).

10.3.1 Name of Statute

The first element is the name of the statute. Use the official short title or popular name, if one exists; otherwise, use "Act of [full date of enactment]" in place of a name. *Do not* use a descriptive name (for example, "An act relating to delinquency charges in retail charge agreements").

The *General and Special Laws of the State of Texas* provides three categories of relevant dates: the dates of relevant legislative action, the date of executive approval, and the date of effectiveness. The date of enactment is the date of the final relevant legislative action on the bill included in the *General and Special Laws*, not the date of executive approval. However, if the date of enactment is not available, use the date of executive approval or date of effectiveness and designate as "Act approved [date]" or "Act effective [date]" instead of "Act of [date]."

10.3.2 Legislature and Session of Enactment

The second element is the legislature and session of enactment. Use the designation "R.S." for a regular session, "1st C.S." for the first called session, and so on. Information about the pre-1876 meetings of the Legislature is included in **Appendix I**.

10.3.3 Chapter and Section Number of Statute

The third element is the chapter and section number of the statute.

A session law that amends existing laws may contain two unrelated sets of section numbers—the amending act itself is divided into sections, each of which may amend various sections of the code. In conformity with the practice of *General and Special Laws of the State of Texas,* distinguish between these two types of section numbers by citing sections of the amending act itself with "§" or "§§" and citing amended code sections with "sec." or "secs."

For example, the amendment to section 31.01 of the Texas Penal Code contained in section 1.01 of the relevant session law is cited as follows:

Act of May 29, 1993, 73d Leg., R.S., ch. 900, § 1.01, sec. 31.01, 1993 Tex. Gen. Laws 3586, 3634 (codified at Tex. Fam. Code § 107.013(c)).

10.3.4 Publication

The fourth element is a citation to *General and Special Laws of the State of Texas* by year and page number. Include both the page on which the act begins and the page on which the cited provision appears, unless the citation is to the entire act:

Tanning Facility Regulation Act, 72d Leg., R.S., ch. 14, § 49, 1991 Tex. Gen. Laws 79.

Act of Jan. 8, 1992, 72d Leg., 3d C.S., ch. 3, § 2(c), 1992 Tex. Gen. Laws 163, 164.

All session laws are published in *General and Special Laws of the State of Texas* ("Tex. Gen. Laws"). If a session law has not yet appeared in *General and Special Laws of the State of Texas,* cite to *Vernon's Texas Session Law Service* ("Tex. Sess. Law Serv.").

Act of May 20, 2013, 83d Leg., R.S., ch. 920, § 4, sec. 981.215(a)(11), 2013 Tex. Sess. Law Serv. 2288, 2289 (to be codified at Tex. Ins. Code § 981.215(a)).

Historical Note

Before 1941, local and special laws in some years were bound separately from the general laws enacted by the same legislature. Cite separate volumes containing both local and special laws as "Tex. Loc. & Spec. Laws," separate volumes containing only special laws as "Tex. Spec. Laws," and so forth. Cite all volumes containing general laws as "Tex. Gen. Laws," whether or not they also contain local and special laws.

10.3.5 Location in Code

If known, a session law's future location in the code or statutes should be appended parenthetically by specifying that the cited session law is to be codified as an amendment to an existing article or code section. The current location of a session law may be noted in a parenthetical if the session law is cited for historical fact of passage or amendment:

Act of May 20, 2013, 83d Leg., R.S., ch. 920, § 4, sec. 981.215(a)(11), 2013 Tex. Sess. Law Serv. 2288, 2289 (to be codified at Tex. Ins. Code § 981.215(a)).

Act of April 11, 1995, 74th Leg., R.S., ch. 19, § 1, sec. 41.001(6)(B), 1995 Tex. Gen. Laws 108, 109 (amended 2003) (current version at Tex. Civ. Prac. & Rem. Code § 41.001(7)).

10.4 Unpublished Statutes

If the statute is too recent to appear in any published source, cite the act according to the rule for session laws (**Rule 10.3**), substituting the bill number for the chapter number. Indicate parenthetically the act's future location in the code, if known:

Act of July 12, 2013, 83d Leg., 2d C.S., H.B. 2, § 2 (to be codified as an amendment to Tex. Health & Safety Code § 171.0031).

10.5 Statutes Available on Electronic Databases

Citations to a statute or session law available from a commercial electronic database, the Texas Legislative Council database, or the Legislative Reference Library of Texas database follow standard citation form:

Tex. Agric. Code § 1.003.

► Practice Tip

The Texas Legislative Council hosts the Texas Constitution, codified statutes, and bills moving through the legislative process on its website. The Legislative Reference Library of Texas publishes session laws.

Cite electronic versions of municipal codes that are also available in print in accordance with **Rule 10.6.1** or **Rule 10.6.2** and append the URL after a comma:

Fort Stockton, Tex., Code of Ordinances, ch. 5, § 5-3 (1987), https://library.municode.com/tx/fort_stockton/codes/code_of_ordinances.

10.6 Municipal Laws and Ordinances

10.6.1 Codified Municipal Laws and Ordinances

Cite codified municipal laws and ordinances analogously to statutes, followed by a parenthetical indicating year of publication. Provide the full political subdivision name (such as the city or county), followed by the state ("Tex."). Then provide the abbreviated name of the local or municipal code, followed by the subdivision or section, and the year of the code:

Hous., Tex., Code of Ordinances ch. 20, art. IV, § 20-216 (1968).

Dallas, Tex., Dallas City Code, ch. 1, § 1-1 (1997).

10.6.2 Uncodified Municipal Laws and Ordinances

If a municipal law or ordinance has not been codified, provide the full political subdivision name (such as the city or county), followed by the state ("Tex."). Then provide the ordinance number or name, and include the exact date of adoption in a parenthetical.

Odessa, Tex., Ordinance 409 (Nov. 12, 1960).

Plano, Tex., Temporary Signs Ordinance (Nov. 14, 2005).

11 Statutes No Longer in Effect

11.1 Repealed, Amended, and Expired Statutes

If a cited statutory provision is no longer in effect because of repeal, amendment, or expiration, cite the official session laws (**Rule 10.3**). Do not cite a repealed, amended, or expired provision to a code, to *Vernon's Annotated Revised Civil Statutes of the State of Texas*, or to an electronic database, even if the provision still appears in one of those sources.

11.1.1 Amended Statutes

(a) **First Citation.** The first citation to a provision that has since been amended must include a parenthetical indicating the year of amendment and a second parenthetical indicating the current code location of the amended version:

Act of July 3, 1984, 68th Leg., 2d C.S., ch. 29, 1984 Tex. Gen. Laws 192 (amended 2001) (current version at Tex. Prop. Code § 21.042(e)).

Or, in the alternative, the first citation may be followed by the phrase "*amended by*" and a full citation to the amending session law:

Act of July 3, 1984, 68th Leg., 2d C.S., ch. 29, 1984 Tex. Gen. Laws 192, *amended by* Act of May 25, 2001, 77th Leg., R.S., ch. 669, § 117, 2001 Tex. Gen. Laws 1244, 1261.

(b) **Subsequent Citations.** Subsequent citations to an amended statute only note the year of amendment parenthetically:

Act of July 3, 1984, 68th Leg., 2d C.S., ch. 29, 1984 Tex. Gen. Laws 192 (amended 2001).

11.1.2 Repealed Statutes

(a) First Citation. Follow the first citation to a provision that has since been repealed with the date of repeal in parentheses. You may also include a full citation to the repealing statute if relevant:

Act of May 30, 1977, 65th Leg., R.S., ch. 817, § 1, sec. 12.01(a), 1977 Tex. Gen. Laws 2039, 2083 (repealed 2003).

Act of May 30, 1977, 65th Leg., R.S., ch. 817, § 1, sec. 12.01(a), 1977 Tex. Gen. Laws 2039, 2083, *repealed by* Act of June 2, 2003, 78th Leg., R.S., ch. 204, § 10.09, 2003 Tex. Gen. Laws 847, 884.

(b) Subsequent Citations. If the first citation to a repealed statute included a full citation to the repealing statute, do not include that information in subsequent citations:

Act of May 30, 1977, 65th Leg., R.S., ch. 817, § 1, sec. 12.01(a), 1977 Tex. Gen. Laws 2039, 2083 (repealed 2003).

11.1.3 Expired Statutes

All citations to a statute that has expired should note the date of expiration parenthetically:

Act of May 31, 2003, 78th Leg., R.S., ch. 1173, § 6, sec. 22.23(c), 2003 Tex. Gen. Laws 3353, 3356 (expired Jan. 1, 2005).

11.2 Statutes Before 1898

Citations to session laws passed before 1898 must include a parallel citation to H.P.N. Gammel's *The Laws of Texas 1822–1897*:

Act approved Mar. 8, 1871, 12th Leg., R.S., ch. 16, § 2, 1871 Tex. Gen. Laws 11, 11, *reprinted in* 6 H.P.N. Gammel, *The Laws of Texas 1822–1897*, at 913, 913 (Austin, Gammel Book Co. 1898).

For information on the dates of pre-1876 legislative sessions, see **Appendix I**. Gammel's collection of the session laws from the first legislative session of the State of Texas in 1846 did not divide them into chapters. Citations to these session laws should therefore omit any reference to chapter numbers.

11.3 Pre-Statehood Statutes and Documents

Laws, treaties, and joint resolutions adopted by the Republic of Texas should be cited to *Laws of the Republic of Texas* ("Repub. Tex. Laws"), with a parallel citation to H.P.N. Gammel's *The Laws of Texas 1822–1897*:

Act approved Dec. 22, 1840, 5th Cong., R.S., § 2, 1841 Repub. Tex. Laws 7, 8, *reprinted in* 2 H.P.N. Gammel, *The Laws of Texas 1822–1897*, at 471, 472 (Austin, Gammel Book Co. 1898).

Other documents from the Republic of Texas and from the colonial period should be cited to Gammel if contained therein:

The Declaration of Independence (Repub. Tex. 1836), at 5, *reprinted in* 1 H.P.N. Gammel, *The Laws of Texas 1822–1897*, at 1063, 1065 (Austin, Gammel Book Co. 1898).

Decree no. 21 (1826) (State of Coahuila & Tex.), *reprinted in* 1 H.P.N. Gammel, *The Laws of Texas 1822–1897*, at 143, 143 (Austin, Gammel Book Co. 1898).

▸ Practice Tip

Although H.P.N. Gammel's compilation of nineteenth-century Texas legal materials was published over a century ago, it remains an important source for many legal materials relating to early Texas history, from colonial times through early statehood.

The University of North Texas has created a free-to-the-public, digital scan of Gammel, which is available on its website.

PART V

QUASI-STATUTORY MATERIAL

12 Comments and Notes Accompanying Statutes

Format Guide

Historical Comment	Tex. Rev. Civ. Stat. Ann. art. 5547-66 cmt. (West 1958).
Revisor's Note	Tex. Agric. Code Ann. § 14.123 revisor's note (West 1982).
U.C.C. Comment	Tex. Bus. & Com. Code Ann. § 2.403 cmt. 2 (West 1968).
Historical Note	Tex. Nat. Res. Code Ann. § 52.024 historical note (West Supp. 1997) [Act of May 22, 1981, 67th Leg., R.S., ch. 438, § 2, 1981 Tex. Gen. Laws 1858, 1859].

12.1 Comments and Revisor's Notes

12.1.1 Historical Comments

► **Practice Tip**

Historical comments are short comments on the purpose and meaning of specific statutes and on the significant departures from predecessor statutes found in older volumes of *Vernon's Annotated Revised Civil Statutes of the State of Texas*. These annotations were gradually removed from recently recompiled volumes of *Vernon's Annotated Revised Civil Statutes* as older civil statutes were repealed and relocated into the subject matter codes. Because the Legislature now rarely creates revised civil statutes, West no longer includes historical comments.

Cite Historical Comments ("cmt.") as follows:

Tex. Rev. Civ. Stat. Ann. art. 5547-66 cmt. (West 1958).

12.1.2 Revisor's Notes

▸ Practice Tip

Some codes in *Vernon's Texas Codes Annotated* include Revisor's Notes, which are comments produced by the Texas Legislative Council that explain changes to the law during codification. These notes are not enacted with the codes but are included as aids to research and interpretation. These notes are often deleted in subsequent editions of the codes as they lose their relevance.

Cite Revisor's Notes ("revisor's note") as follows:

Tex. Agric. Code Ann. § 14.123 revisor's note (West 1982).

12.1.3 U.C.C. Comments

▸ Practice Tip

Vernon's Texas Business and Commerce Code Annotated includes the comments to the Uniform Commercial Code, prepared by the American Law Institute and the National Conference of Commissioners on Uniform State Laws.

Cite U.C.C. Comments ("cmt. [*x*]") as follows:

Tex. Bus. & Com. Code Ann. § 1.307 cmt. 2 (West 2009).

12.2 Historical Notes

▸ Practice Tip

Sections of session laws dealing with the act's date of effectiveness or the act's applicability to certain transactions will often be codified as Historical Notes and placed outside of the main text of the statute.

When citing Historical Notes ("historical note"), indicate their origin by providing in brackets a session law citation to the appropriate section of the enacted bill (see **Rule 10.3**):

Tex. Nat. Res. Code Ann. § 52.024 historical note (West Supp. 1997) [Act of May 22, 1981, 67th Leg., R.S., ch. 438, § 2, 1981 Tex. Gen. Laws 1858, 1859].

13 Rules of Procedure and Evidence

Format Guide

Rules of Procedure	Tex. R. Civ. P. 97(d).
Rules of Judicial Administration	Tex. R. Jud. Admin. 5, *reprinted in* Tex. Gov't Code Ann., tit. 2, subtit. F app.
Rules of Appellate Procedure	Tex. R. App. P. 2.
Rules of Evidence	Tex. R. Evid. 405(b).
Local Court Rules	Dallas (Tex.) Civ. Dist. Ct. Loc. R. 1.22.

Appendix H provides a list of rules currently in force along with their abbreviations for quick reference.

13.1 Rules of Procedure

13.1.1 Rules of Civil Procedure Currently in Force

If a rule of civil procedure is currently in force, cite the rule without indicating the date of publication:

Tex. R. Civ. P. 97(d).

13.1.2 Rules of Civil Procedure No Longer in Force

Cite rules no longer in force as per **Rule 13.1.1**, but add: a citation to a source where the text of the rule may be found, which includes the volume, source name (e.g., "Tex. B.J."), and the page on which the rule appears; a date parenthetical, which includes the promulgating court's name, the dates of adoption and repeal; and, if particularly relevant, a full citation to the repealing or amending statute or order. Possible sources for locating the text of old rules include the *Texas Reports, Texas Criminal Reports, Texas Register, Texas Bar Journal,* or *South Western Reporter (Texas Cases)*:

Tex. Sup. Ct. R. 8, 32 Tex. 809 (1871, superseded 1877).

Tex. R. Crim. Post Trial & App. P. 306, 44 Tex. B.J. 900 (Tex. Crim. App. 1981, repealed 1986).

Citation may also be made to the session law (if legislatively enacted, cited as a statute no longer in effect per **Rule 11.1**) or rule collection (if promulgated by a court, cited per **Rule 13.1.1**, with the addition of a date parenthetical) in which the rule appears; however, the above sources are more readily available and thus preferred:

Tex. R. Civ. P. 195 (Vernon 1941, repealed 1957).

Act approved May 13, 1846, 1st Leg., § 55, 1846 Tex. Gen. Laws 363, 376, *reprinted in* 2 H.P.N. Gammel, *The Laws of Texas 1822–1897*, at 1669, 1682 (Austin, Gammel Book Co. 1898), *repealed by* Rules of Practice Act, 46th Leg., R.S., ch. 25, § 1, 1939 Tex. Gen. Laws 201, 201.

When citing Republic of Texas court rules and early State of Texas court rules consult **Appendix K.1**.

13.1.3 Commentaries on Rules of Civil Procedure

Cite the commentaries on the Rules of Civil Procedure by author and title. Include also a parenthetical statement with the publisher and date of publication:

Robert W. Calvert, *The Application for Writ of Error*, Tex. R. Civ. P. Ann. 469 (West 1985).

13.1.4 Rules of Judicial Administration

► Practice Tip

The Rules of Judicial Administration are promulgated by the Texas Supreme Court and govern the administrative tasks that state judges must fulfill. They are reprinted as an appendix to Title 2, Subtitle F of the Texas Government Code in *Vernon's Texas Codes Annotated.*

The first citation to these rules must include a direction to their location in the Texas Government Code:

Tex. R. Jud. Admin. 5, *reprinted in* Tex. Gov't Code Ann., tit. 2, subtit. F app.

In subsequent citations, omit this citation to the Government Code:

Tex. R. Jud. Admin. 5.

13.2 Rules of Appellate Procedure

Historical Note

The Texas Supreme Court and the Texas Court of Criminal Appeals jointly promulgated the Texas Rules of Appellate Procedure in 1986. The Courts later promulgated a new and reorganized set of Rules of Appellate Procedure in 1997. The 1997 rules are the basis for the current Rules of Appellate Procedure.

13.2.1 Current Rules of Appellate Procedure

The Texas Rules of Appellate Procedure are published annually in a special pamphlet accompanying *Vernon's Texas Rules Annotated.* Cite the current Texas Rules of Appellate Procedure as follows:

Tex. R. App. P. 2.

13.2.2 Texas Rules of Appellate Procedure No Longer in Force

The *Texas Bar Journal* is the publication of record for newly promulgated rules. Because rules of appellate procedure that are no longer in effect may be otherwise difficult to locate, cite such rules to the volume and page of the *Texas Bar Journal* in which they first appeared.

Cite a Texas Rule of Appellate Procedure no longer in force according to **Rule 13.2.1**, but also include: a citation to the *Texas Bar Journal* by volume, publication title ("Tex. B.J."), and the page on which the rule appears; and a parenthetical including the court that promulgated the rule (the Texas Supreme Court, the Court of Criminal Appeals, or both), the date of promulgation, and the date of amendment or repeal:

Tex. R. App. P. 9, 49 Tex. B.J. 561 (Tex. & Tex. Crim. App. 1986, amended 1997).

13.2.3 Texas Rules of Appellate Procedure—Appendix for Criminal Cases

Before September 1, 1997, four rules were published as an appendix to the Texas Rules of Appellate Procedure for use only in criminal cases. Cite these rules according to **Rule 13.2.2**, but replace "Tex. R. App. P." with "Tex. R. App. P. Crim. app.":

Tex. R. App. P. Crim. app. 2.

13.3 Rules of Evidence

Historical Note

The Texas Rules of Evidence, effective since March 1, 1998, are jointly promulgated by the Texas Supreme Court and the Texas Court of Criminal Appeals.

Cite Texas Rules of Evidence as follows:

Tex. R. Evid. 405(b).

For guidance on citing pre-1998 rules of civil and criminal evidence, see **Appendix K.2** and **K.3**.

13.4 Local Court Rules

Local court rules vary considerably. Generally, citations must indicate at least the court, location, type of rule ("Loc. R."), and rule number. Other helpful information may be added parenthetically:

13th Tex. App. (Corpus Christi) Loc. R. 1.

Dallas (Tex.) Civ. Dist. Ct. Loc. R. 1.22.

220th (Tex.) Dist. Ct. Loc. R. 1.6 (Bosque, Comanche, and Hamilton Counties).

14 Legislative History

Format Guide

Unenacted Bills	Tex. S.B. 357, 78th Leg., R.S. (2003).
Concurrent & Joint Resolutions	Tex. H.R. Con. Res. 173, 69th Leg., R.S., 1985 Tex. Gen. Laws 3574 (energy conservation resolution).
House and Senate Journals	S.J. of Tex., 69th Leg., R.S. 481 (1985).
Fiscal Notes & Bill Analyses	Fiscal Note, Tex. H.B. 276, 83d Leg., R.S. (2013).
House and Senate Rules	Tex. S. Rule 2.01(a), S. Res. 5, 83d Leg., R.S., 2013 S.J. of Tex. 26, 26, *reprinted in Rules of the Senate,* Texas Legislative Manual 4 (2013).
Veto Messages	Veto Message of Gov. Clements, Tex. S.B. 753, 66th Leg., R.S. (1979).
Gubernatorial Proclamations	Tex. Gov. Proclamation No. 41-2295, 71st Leg., R.S., ch. 1263, 1989 Tex. Gen. Laws 5840.

14.1 Bills and Resolutions

14.1.1 Unenacted Bills

Cite unenacted bills of the Texas Legislature by bill number, legislature number and session, and year. Use the designation "R.S." for "regular session" and the designation "C.S." for "called session":

Tex. S.B. 357, 78th Leg., R.S. (2003).

Tex. H.B. 13, 79th Leg., 2d C.S. (2005).

14.1.2 Concurrent and Joint Resolutions

(a) Enacted Resolutions. If codified, a resolution should be cited as a statute per **Rule 10.2.1**. If the resolution is uncodified or cited to document legislative history, then it should be cited as a session law to the *General and Special Laws of the State of Texas* per **Rule 10.3**. When cited as a session law, the citation may include a descriptive parenthetical, if useful to the reader:

Tex. S. Con. Res. 4, 65th Leg., R.S., 1977 Tex. Gen. Laws 3177 (Taft-Hartley Resolution).

Tex. H.R. Con. Res. 173, 69th Leg., R.S., 1985 Tex. Gen. Laws 3574 (energy conservation resolution).

Tex. S.J. Res. 3, 65th Leg., R.S., 1977 Tex. Gen. Laws 3353 (proposing a constitutional amendment relating to the denial of bail).

(b) Unenacted Resolutions. Cite unenacted resolutions according to **Rule 14.1.1**:

Tex. H.R.J. Res. 1, 79th Leg., R.S. (2005).

14.2 House and Senate Journals

▸ Practice Tip

The House and Senate Journals are the official records of the proceedings of each chamber. They do not contain transcripts of the debates in either house but may contain information such as bill histories, text of bill amendments, floor votes for each bill, addresses and speeches to the legislature, and messages from the governor to the legislature.

Journal citations must specify the chamber, legislature number and session, page, and year; include additional relevant information parenthetically:

H.J. of Tex., 66th Leg., R.S. 4423 (1979).

S.J. of Tex., 69th Leg., R.S. 481 (1985).

S.J. of Tex., 68th Leg., 2d C.S. 17 (1984) (address of H. Ross Perot).

14.3 Fiscal Notes and Bill Analyses

▸ Practice Tip

Rules of the Texas House of Representatives require that certain bills be accompanied by "fiscal notes" (authored by the Legislative Budget Board), "bill analyses" (written by each committee to report on the bill), or both. In addition, since 1986 the Senate has prepared bill analyses for selected bills. These documents are located in the original bill file for each bill. Bill files are kept in the Legislative Reference Library located in the State Capitol Building or, in the case of bills before 1973, in the Archives Division of the Texas State Library in Austin. Bill analyses and fiscal notes are also available on Texas Legislature Online.

Citations to bill analyses must first include the name of the committee that authored the analysis. (This is omitted for fiscal notes because the Legislative Budget Board is always the author.) Citations to both must then include the title of the document ("Fiscal Note" or "Bill Analysis") and a full citation to the bill to which they are attached (**Rule 14.1.1**): If a committee has issued more than one analysis for a bill, include a parenthetical with the bill version and the full date of the analysis:

Fiscal Note, Tex. H.B. 276, 83d Leg., R.S. (2013).

House Comm. on Civ. Practices, Bill Analysis, Tex. H.B. 744, 79th Leg., R.S. (2005).

S. Comm. on Educ., Bill Analysis, Tex. S.B. 1365, 87th Leg., R.S. (as filed, Mar. 23, 2021).

Committee names should be abbreviated per *The Bluebook* Tables T6, T9, and T10.

14.4 Committee Minutes

▸ Practice Tip

Most standing committees of the Legislature prepare minutes of their meetings. Senate committee minutes since 1973 may be found at the Legislative Reference Library. House committee minutes from as early as 1960 are located in the Office of the House Committee Coordinator. And Senate and House committee minutes, beginning with the 75th Session, are available on Texas Legislature Online.

Committee minutes must be cited by committee, page number, legislature number and session, and exact date of the meeting:

Tex. S. Comm. on Jurisprudence Minutes 2, 83d Leg., R.S. (May 17, 2013).

14.5 Testimony and Debate

▸ Practice Tip

Since 1973, testimony presented in public hearings and debate on the floor of each house has been recorded on audiotape. Information concerning House tapes is available through the Office of the House Committee Coordinator; Senate tapes through Senate Staff Services. Tapes are also available through the media offices of the Legislative Reference Library.

Legislative testimony and debates are cited to the transcripts of such tapes. Include as much of the following information as is pertinent: title of act, nature of proceeding (hearing, debate, etc.), bill number, house or committee involved, legislature number and session, page number of transcript, and exact date of proceeding. In addition, include parenthetically any information that would be helpful in locating the transcript:

Debate on Tex. S.B. 1247 on the Floor of the Senate, 81st Leg., R.S. 1–7 (Feb. 18, 2009) (transcript available from Senate Staff Services Office).

Cite the tapes themselves only if transcripts are not available. Indicate parenthetically where the tapes may be found:

The Texas Deceptive Trade Practices–Consumer Protection Act: Hearings on Tex. H.B. 417 Before the House Comm. on Bus. & Indus., 63d Leg., R.S. (May 21, 1973) (statement of Attorney General Hill) (tape available from the House Video/Audio Services Office).

14.6 House and Senate Rules

▸ Practice Tip

Each house of the legislature adopts rules at the beginning of each legislative session. The rules are adopted by House or Senate resolutions that are printed in the House and Senate Journals and are reprinted in the *Texas Legislative Manual*. The current legislative rules are available online on the respective websites of the House and Senate.

Citations to the House and Senate rules must specify the house, rule number, resolution number, legislature number and session, year, journal, the first page on which the rules appear, and the exact page on which the cited rule appears. If either house merely adopts the rules from a previous year without republishing the full text of the rules in its journal, add a parallel citation to the location of the rule in the *Texas Legislative Manual*. Otherwise, citation to the *Texas Legislative Manual* is optional:

Tex. H.R. Rule 1, § (9)(b), Tex. H.R. 4, 83d Leg., R.S., 2013 H.J. of Tex. 53, 55, *reprinted in Rules of the House*, Texas Legislative Manual 5 (2013).

Tex. S. Rule 2.01(a), S. Res. 5, 83d Leg., R.S., 2013 S.J. of Tex. 26, 26, *reprinted in Rules of the Senate*, Texas Legislative Manual 4 (2013).

14.6.1 Joint House and Senate Rules

The House and Senate have sometimes adopted joint rules. Joint rules are adopted by a joint resolution that is printed in the session laws. Citations must specify the rule number, resolution number, legislature number and session, year, and page number. Citation to the *Texas Legislative Manual* is optional:

Tex. Leg. J. Rules 14, Tex. S.C.R. 7, 55th Leg., R.S., 1957 Tex. Gen. Laws 1499, *reprinted in Joint Rules of the Two Houses*, Texas Legislative Manual 461, 465 (1957).

14.7 Gubernatorial Messages

▸ Practice Tip

Veto messages and other messages concerning legislation from the Office of the Governor are printed in the legislative journals if delivered while the legislature is in session. Otherwise, the message may be found in the original bill file.

14.7.1 Veto Messages

Citations of veto messages should include a title ("Veto Message") with the governor's name, a citation to the bill vetoed in accordance with **Rule 14.1.1**, and a citation to the house or senate Journal, if the message appears in one, in accordance with **Rule 14.2**. Include the year parenthetically:

Veto Message of Gov. Clements, Tex. S.B. 452, S.J. of Tex., 71st Leg., R.S. 3631 (1989).

Veto Message of Gov. Clements, Tex. S.B. 753, 66th Leg., R.S. (1979).

14.7.2 Gubernatorial Proclamations and Messages

Gubernatorial proclamations that call for special sessions or veto general appropriations bills may be cited by reference to the Texas

Register, the Senate Journal, or the *General and Special Laws of the State of Texas* in order of preference. Citations to the Texas Register must be made in accordance with **Rule 16.1.2**. Citations to the Senate Journal must be made in accordance with **Rule 14.2**. Citations to the *General and Special Laws of the State of Texas* must be made in accordance with **Rule 10.3.4**:

Tex. Gov. Proclamation No. 41-2295, 71st Leg., R.S., ch. 1263, 1989 Tex. Gen. Laws 5840.

The Gov. of the State of Tex., Proclamation 41-3844, 46 Tex. Reg 3984 (2021).

Tex. Gov. Proclamation, Tex. S.B. 1, S.J. of Tex., 87th Leg., R.S. 3191 (2021).

Tex. Gov. Proclamation No. 41-3844, 87th Leg., R.S., ch. 1053, 2021 Tex. Gen. Laws 3777.

Other gubernatorial proclamations and messages are cited according to **Rule 16.1.2(e)**.

▸ Practice Tip

Gubernatorial proclamations and messages are printed in several locations. Many gubernatorial messages, proclamations, and executive orders are printed in the Texas Register. Proclamations designating emergency items are printed in the legislative journals. Proclamations vetoing or line-item vetoing Senate bills are reprinted in the Senate Journal, but the House Journal simply lists the items vetoed or line-item vetoed. Proclamations that line-item veto the general appropriations act are printed in the *General and Special Laws of the State of Texas* immediately following the text of the General Appropriations Act. Executive orders, proclamations, speeches of the governor, and veto messages are also available online from the Legislative Reference Library of Texas.

15 Formal Advisory Opinions

Format Guide

Attorney General Opinions After 1938	Tex. Att'y Gen. Op. Nos. WW-224 (1957), S-76 (1953), V-722 (1948).
Attorney General Letter Opinions or Advisories	Tex. Att'y Gen. LA-157, 2 (1978).
Attorney General ORLs	Tex. Att'y Gen. OR2002-6816.
Secretary of State Advisory Opinions	Tex. Sec'y State Op. No. JH-2, 1 (1991).
Texas Ethics Commission Opinions	Tex. Ethics Comm'n Op. No. 3 (1992).

15.1 Attorney General

15.1.1 Attorney General Opinions

▸ Practice Tip

The proper form for citing opinions of Texas attorneys general varies depending on the date on which the opinion was issued. A consecutive numbering system was adopted for all opinions issued after 1938. Opinions issued since then have been prefaced by the letter "O" from 1939 to 1946; by the letter "V" from 1947 to 1952; and since 1953, by the initial or initials of the attorney general issuing the opinion. Attorney

General Opinions since 1939 are available online through the attorney general's website.

(a) **Opinions Issued After 1938.** Citation to Attorney General Opinions are by the designation ("Tex. Att'y Gen. Op."), the Attorney General's initial or initials followed by a hyphen, opinion number, and a parenthetical indicating the year. String citations are arranged with the most recent opinion first:

Tex. Att'y Gen. Op. No. GA-0002 (2002).

Tex. Att'y Gen. Op. Nos. WW-224 (1957), S-76 (1953), V-722 (1948).

(b) **Opinions Issued Before 1939.** Opinions issued before 1939 have no standardized numbering system. Citation to these opinions must include the designation ("Tex. Att'y Gen. Op."), a parenthetical including the name of the official to whom the opinion is directed and the exact date of the opinion, and a citation to the *Biennial Report of the Attorney General of the State of Texas*, which includes the volume, the title ("Tex. Att'y Gen. Biennial Rep."), the first page of the opinion, and the exact page on which the cited material appears:

Tex. Att'y Gen. Op. (To Hon. J.H. Walker, Aug. 21, 1929), 1928–1930 Tex. Att'y Gen. Biennial Rep. 163, 174.

15.1.2 Attorney General Letter Opinions or Letter Advisories Issued Before January 4, 1999

On January 4, 1999, Attorney General John Cornyn discontinued the practice of issuing Letter Opinions and Letter Advisories. All Attorney General Opinions are now issued under the attorney general's initials, and these opinions are cited as shown in **Rule 15.1.1**.

Cite the pre-1999 Letter Opinions and Letter Advisories by the attorney general according to **Rule 15.1.1**, but omit the designation "Op." and preface the decision numbers by the letters "LO" ("Letter Opinion") or "LA" ("Letter Advisory") followed by a hyphen, the opinion or advisory number, and a parenthetical indicating the year of issue:

Tex. Att'y Gen. LO-92-002 (1992).

Tex. Att'y Gen. LA-157 (1978).

15.1.3 Attorney General Open Records Letter Rulings (ORLs)

Cite to Open Records Letter Rulings (ORLs) by the designation "OR," proceeded by the letter ruling number (the year, a hyphen, and the letter number). Note there is no space or punctuation between "OR" and the year:

Tex. Att'y Gen. OR2002-6816.

15.2 Secretary of State

The Secretary of State is authorized to issue advisory opinions on state election laws. Citations to such opinions are by the designation ("Tex. Sec'y State Op."), the secretary's initial or initials followed by a hyphen, the opinion number, and the year. String citations are arranged with the most recent opinion first:

Tex. Sec'y State Op. No. JH-2 (1991).

Tex. Sec'y State Op. Nos. AOG-2 (1997), AOG-1 (1996), GSB-5, GSB-4 (1990).

15.3 Texas Ethics Commission

The Texas Ethics Commission is authorized to issue advisory opinions on the application of specific statutes. Opinions are cited by opinion number and year:

Tex. Ethics Comm'n Op. No. 3 (1992).

16 Agency Material

Format Guide

Codified Rules	9 Tex. Reg. 982, 982 (2014) (to be codified at 16 Tex. Admin. Code § 33.13) (proposed Oct. 25, 2013) (Tex. Alcoholic Beverages Comm'n, Application Procedures), *proposed by* 38 Tex. Reg. 7403, 7404 (2013).
Emergency Rules	33 Tex. Reg. 7653, 7653–54 (2008) (emerg. amend. to 4 Tex. Admin. Code §§ 19.411, 19.413) (adopted Sept. 12, 2008, expired Dec. 24, 2008) (Tex. Dep't Agric., Quarantined Areas; Restrictions).
Other *Texas Register* Material	Office of the Att'y Gen., Tex. Health & Safety Code Settlement Notice, 31 Tex. Reg. 5691, 5693 (2006).
Administrative Orders	Tex. Pub. Util. Comm'n, Application of Southwestern Bell Telephone Company for Authority to Implement Private Coin Service, Docket No. 5905, 10 Tex. P.U.C. Bull. 1424, 1426 (Mar. 8, 1985) (final order granting application).
Reports, Studies, and Bulletins	53 Tex. Educ. Agency Biennial Rep. 17 (1984).

16.1 Administrative Rules and Regulations

Historical Note

In 1975, the Texas Legislature passed the Administrative Procedure and Texas Register Act, which provides for the publication of all proposed and adopted state administrative rules, regulations, and other related information in the *Texas Register*. In 1977 the Texas Legislature passed the Texas Administrative Code Act, which requires the compilation and indexing of administrative rules.

Today, proposed rules and regulations first appear chronologically in the weekly *Texas Register* along with their proposed *Texas Administrative Code* citations. If the rules are adopted, the *Texas Register* reports their adoption and any changes from the rules as initially proposed and published. The rules are then compiled into the next annual supplement of the appropriate title of the *Texas Administrative Code*. The numbered titles of the *Texas Administrative Code* are broad categories into which the state agencies are grouped (e.g., Health Services, Natural Resources and Conservation, Public Finance).

The *Texas Register* and *Texas Administrative Code* are both available through the Texas Secretary of State's website.

16.1.1 *Texas Administrative Code*

Whenever possible, cite Texas administrative rules and regulations to the *Texas Administrative Code* ("Tex. Admin. Code") by title, part, chapter, section, and year of the bound volume. The title number precedes "Tex. Admin. Code," while the remaining divisions follow "Tex. Admin. Code." Citations may optionally include a parenthetical indicating the agency or organization issuing the rule and the subject heading of the rule. Abbreviate agencies in accordance with *The Bluebook* Tables T6 and T10:

4 Tex. Admin. Code pt. 1 ch. 9 subch. F § 12 (2013) (Tex. Dep't of Agric., Seed Sampling Procedures).

(a) **Rules Adopted or Amended After the Date of the Most Recent Texas Administrative Code.** Cite rules adopted or amended after the date of the most recent annual *Texas Administrative Code* to the *Texas Register* under **Rule 16.1.2**.

(b) Rules No Longer in Force. For rules no longer in force, cite to either the *Texas Register* or the *Texas Administrative Code*, but include the designation "*repealed by*" followed by a full citation to the repealing rule in the *Texas Register* under **Rule 16.1.2**:

19 Tex. Admin. Code § 89.1260 (2006) (Tex. Educ. Agency, Monitoring of Programs and Enforcing Law and Commissioner's Rules), *repealed by* 32 Tex. Reg. 3825, 3826 (2007), *adopted by* 32 Tex. Reg. 6311, 6311 (2007).

16.1.2 *Texas Register*

When citing proposed rules in the *Texas Register*, provide the volume, the publication name ("Tex. Reg."), the page at which the rule begins, the exact page of the cited material, and the year in which the cited volume was published. In addition, cite parenthetically the location in the *Texas Administrative Code* where the rule is to be codified (see **Rule 16.1.2(a)**). A separate parenthetical must also include the name of the agency or organization proposing the rule and, if useful for clarity, either the title of the proposed rule or, when citing multiple sections, the narrowest subject heading that applies to all cited sections. If particularly relevant, the exact date the rule was proposed may also be included in a separate parenthetical:

39 Tex. Reg. 982, 982 (2014) (to be codified at 16 Tex. Admin. Code § 33.13) (proposed Oct. 25, 2013) (Tex. Alcoholic Beverages Comm'n, Application Procedures), *proposed by* 38 Tex. Reg. 7403, 7404 (2013).

39 Tex. Reg. 573, 574 (2014) (to be codified at 22 Tex. Admin. Code § 367.14) (proposed Feb. 7, 2014) (Tex. State Bd. Plumbing Exam'rs, Contested Case; State Office of Admin. Hearings).

Unless otherwise noted within this rule, abbreviations for *Texas Register* citations should be in accordance with *The Bluebook* Tables T6, T9, T10, and T12.

(a) Location in the *Texas Administrative Code*. The parenthetical citation to the *Texas Administrative Code* should indicate whether the rule is newly codified ("to be codified at") or merely an amendment to an existing rule ("to be codified as an amendment to"):

39 Tex. Reg. 557, 558 (2014) (to be codified as an amendment to 1 Tex. Admin. Code § 353.405) (Tex. Health & Human Servs. Comm'n, Marketing).

(b) Amendments to Proposed Rules. The *Texas Register* will report adoption of, or proposed changes to, previously proposed rules. If a previously proposed rule has been amended since its proposal and is to be adopted as amended, then the full, amended text of the rule will be printed with the notification of its adoption. In this case, cite to the text as published with the adoption notice. The previous publication of the originally proposed text need not be cited.

However, if a rule is adopted unchanged, the text will not be reprinted on the page at which it is adopted in the *Texas Register*. It will be necessary to cite to both the page at which it is proposed—at which the text of the rule is located—and the page at which it is adopted in the *Texas Register*.

First, cite the location at which it is proposed followed by the designation "*adopted by*" and a full citation to the adopting provision under **Rule 16.1.2**:

38 Tex. Reg. 8492, 8493 (2013), *adopted by* 39 Tex. Reg. 623, 623 (2014) (to be codified as an amendment to 10 Tex. Admin. Code § 1.10) (Tex. Dep't of Hous. & Cmty. Affairs, Public Comment Procedures).

(c) Emergency Rules.

▸ **Practice Tip**

Emergency rules are rules adopted to prevent imminent peril to the public and are effective without notice for a maximum period of 180 days. Emergency rules are not codified in the *Texas Administrative Code* but typically amend, repeal, or add a temporary section to the Code. Emergency rules are published in the *Texas Register*.

Cite an emergency rule per **Rule 16.1.2**, adding a parenthetical following the year of the *Texas Register* in which the rule appears that indicates the emergency rule's location in and its relationship to the *Texas Administrative Code,* whether it amends ("emerg. amend."), repeals ("emerg. repeal"), or adds a new section to ("emerg. rule") the affected code portion. The dates of adoption and expiration are listed in a second parenthetical:

31 Tex. Reg. 6157, 6157–58 (2006) (emerg. rule 16 Tex. Admin. Code § 25.50) (adopted Aug. 4, 2006, expired Nov. 17, 2006) (Pub. Util. Comm'n of Tex., Suspension of Disconnection of Electric Service During Summer 2006).

33 Tex. Reg. 7653, 7653–54 (2008) (emerg. amend. to 4 Tex. Admin. Code §§ 19.411, 19.413) (adopted Sept. 12, 2008, expired Dec. 24, 2008) (Tex. Dep't Agric., Quarantined Areas; Restrictions).

15 Tex. Reg. 2075, 2075 (1990) (emerg. repeal of 28 Tex. Admin. Code §§ 64.5, 64.10, 64.15, 64.20) (adopted Apr. 4, 1990, expired Aug. 2, 1990) (Tex. Workers' Comp. Comm'n, Requirement for Written Contract; Attorney Fees; Expenses; Disbursement Statement).

In the same issue of the *Texas Register,* a rule may be adopted on an emergency basis and proposed as a permanent rule. If the rule is permanently adopted unchanged, the text will not be reprinted. When citing such a rule, analogize to **Rule 16.1.2(b)**: the emergency rule is first cited, followed thereafter by a citation to the location in the *Texas Register* where the emergency rule was proposed as a permanent rule, followed by the location in the *Texas Register* at which the rule is adopted as a permanent rule. That string is then followed by a parenthetical indicating the location of the affected section of the *Texas Administrative Code* and a separate parenthetical indicating the agency name and, if useful for clarity, either the title of the proposed rule or, when citing multiple sections, the narrowest subject heading that applies to all cited sections:

34 Tex. Reg. 6202, 6206–08 (2009) (emerg. rule), *proposed by* 35 Tex. Reg. 181, 181, 197–201 (2010), *adopted by* 35 Tex. Reg. 2160, 2160, 2172–74 (2010) (codified at 28 Tex. Admin. Code §§ 5.4902–.4908, 5.4911), *amended by* 36 Tex. Reg. 9331, 9333–34 (2011) (codified as an amendment to 28 Tex. Admin. Code §§ 5.4903, 5.4905) (Tex. Dep't of Ins.).

(d) Rules No Longer in Force. Rules no longer in force are cited according to **Rule 16.1.2**. This citation should be followed by a full citation to the amending or repealing rule and a parenthetical indicating the former section of the *Texas Administrative Code* at which the rule was codified. Indicate whether the original rule was amended or repealed before the citation to the amending or repealing rule:

10 Tex. Reg. 4562, 4562–64 (1985), *adopted by* 11 Tex. Reg. 126, 126 (1986), *repealed in part and amended in part by* 11 Tex. Reg. 2408, 2408–11 (1986) (emerg. rule), *proposed by* 11 Tex. Reg. 2412, 2412–13 (1986), *adopted by* 11 Tex. Reg. 3258, 3258 (1986), *repealed by* 24 Tex. Reg. 6965, 6965–66 (1999) (former 1 Tex. Admin. Code §§ 71.41–.48) (Tex. Sec'y of State).

(e) Other Materials Found in the *Texas Register*. The *Texas Register* is required by statute to publish a variety of materials beyond administrative rules, including executive orders, attorney general opinions, and other agency materials, like applications, proposals, and notices. When citing such material, include its title or a description indicating its nature, along with the volume of the *Texas Register*, the first page of the material, the exact page on which the cited text appears, and the year:

Office of the Att'y Gen., Tex. Health & Safety Code Settlement Notice, 31 Tex. Reg. 5691, 5691 (2006).

The Tex. A & M Univ. Sys., Notice of Sale of Oil, Gas, & Sulphur Lease, 33 Tex. Reg. 7792, 7792 (2008).

The Governor of the State of Tex., Appointments for June 26, 2006, 31 Tex. Reg. 5427, 5427 (2006).

Abbreviate the title or description in accordance with *The Bluebook* Tables T6, T9, T10, T11, and T12.

16.1.3 Rules Promulgated Before 1976

Historical Note

Rules promulgated by administrative agencies before January 1, 1976, do not appear in the *Texas Register*. Official copies of these rules and regulations are on file at the offices of the respective agencies.

Before 1976, administrative rules were identified by a ten-digit number divided into four units by decimal points. In 1977, with the advent of the *Texas Administrative Code*, this numbering system fell into disuse. It is increasingly difficult to locate rules using their former ten-digit identifier, so even if a rule bears one, it should be cited as indicated below.

Rules promulgated before 1976 are cited by agency and date of adoption. Cite such a rule according to the promulgating agency's identification system, followed by a parenthetical indicating the rule's repeal and the date of that repeal. Include any information that would help a reader find the rule parenthetically:

Tex. R.R. Comm'n, Rule 400b (1964) (repealed 1976) (on file with the Texas Railroad Commission).

16.2 Administrative Orders

Cite orders of state agencies by name of the agency or commission, title of the adjudication or order, docket or order number, and a parenthetical indicating the exact date. A parenthetical noting the disposition of the cause may follow the date parenthetical. If agency opinions are published in a series, include a citation to this publication by volume, title, page, and date. If the order was issued by a particular division of the agency, indicate the division in the date parenthetical. Abbreviate using the following conventions: agency names and divisions in accordance with *The Bluebook* Tables T6 and T10; dates in accordance with *The Bluebook* Table T12; and agency publications in accordance with *The Bluebook* Table T13. Agency publications with a common abbreviation in

Texas, but not found in *The Bluebook*, may nevertheless be abbreviated. For example, the Texas Public Utility Commission Bulletin is often abbreviated "Tex. P.U.C. Bull." and may be cited as such. The title of an adjudication, however, is not abbreviated:

Tex. Pub. Util. Comm'n, *Application of Southwestern Bell Telephone Company for Authority to Implement Private Coin Service*, Docket No. 5905, 10 Tex. P.U.C. Bull. 1424, 1426 (Mar. 8, 1985) (final order granting application).

Tex. R.R. Comm'n, *Enforcement Action Against Westco Gas, Inc. for Violations of the Texas Administrative Code, Utilities Code, and Pipeline Safety Regulations*, Docket No. 8983, Gas Util. Info. Bull. No. 713, 3 (Gas Servs. Div. Dec. 3, 2002) (proposed final order).

16.3 Reports, Studies, and Bulletins

▸ Practice Tip

Publications of state agencies (e.g., reports, studies, newsletters, and bulletins) are collected and processed by the Texas State Publications Clearinghouse and are available for loan from the Reference Room of the Texas State Library. Most documents are available in microfiche format from the Records Management Division of the Texas State Library. Selected publications are distributed to depository libraries, which are located in many of the major academic and public libraries throughout the state. Agency publications may also be available online.

Cite reports, studies, and bulletins published by administrative agencies in pamphlet form as a book, in accordance with **Rule 18.1**.

16.3.1 Pamphlets of Limited Circulation

Cite pamphlets of limited circulation per **Rule 18.1**, but include the exact date if available and parenthetically add any information that might be helpful in locating the source:

Bob McKay, Location of High Technology Industry in Texas: A Critical Assessment 6 (June 1984) (Tex. Econ. Dev. Comm'n).

16.3.2 Governmental Agencies and Institutional Authors

Cite governmental agencies and institutional authors like any other author.

Governor's Advisory Panel on Offshore Oil and Chemical Spill Responses, Final Report 47 (Feb. 1985).

16.3.3 Annual and Regular Reports

Cite annual and regular reports by volume number, agency name and report name, the exact page of the cited material, and a date parenthetical:

53 Tex. Educ. Agency Biennial Rep. 17 (1984).

17 State Bar Materials

Format Guide

State Bar Rules	Tex. State Bar R. art. III, § 2, *reprinted in* Tex. Gov't Code Ann., tit. 2, subtit. G, app. A.
Disciplinary Rules of Professional Conduct	Tex. Disciplinary Rules Prof'l Conduct R. 1.02(a)(2), *reprinted in* Tex. Gov't Code Ann., tit. 2, subtit. G, app. A (Tex. State Bar R. art. X, § 9).
Ethics Opinions	Tex. Comm. on Prof'l Ethics, Op. 593, 73 Tex. B.J. 254, 255 (2010).
Rules of Disciplinary Procedure	Tex. Rules Disciplinary P. R. 2.16(A), *reprinted in* Tex. Gov't Code Ann., tit. 2, subtit. G, app. A-1.
Code of Judicial Conduct	Tex. Code Jud. Conduct, Canon 2(A), *reprinted in* Tex. Gov't Code Ann., tit. 2, subtit. G, app. B.
Advisory Opinions	Comm. on Jud. Ethics, State Bar of Tex., Op. 139 (1991), *reprinted in* 63 Tex. Jud. Council & Off. Ct. Admin. Tex. Jud. Sys. Ann. Rep. 121 (1991).

17.1 State Bar Rules

▸ Practice Tip

The Texas Supreme Court promulgated the State Bar Rules in 1940. These rules are reprinted as Appendix A to Title 2, Subtitle G of the Texas Government Code in *Vernon's Texas Codes Annotated.*

For information on citing former Canons of Ethics, the former Texas Code of Professional Responsibility, and other rules no longer in force see **Appendix K.4**.

For a state bar rule currently in force, cite the rule by title ("Tex. State Bar R."), article, and section. In the initial citation to this rule, indicate the location of the rule in the Texas Government Code Annotated:

Tex. State Bar R. art. III, § 2, *reprinted in* Tex. Gov't Code Ann., tit. 2, subtit. G, app. A.

Tex. State Bar R. art. IV, § 5(A)(1), *reprinted in* Tex. Gov't Code Ann., tit. 2, subtit. G, app. A.

17.1.1 Short Form

Subsequent citations of state bar rules may omit the reference to the Texas Government Code Annotated:

Tex. State Bar R. art. III, § 2.

17.2 Texas Disciplinary Rules of Professional Conduct

▸ Practice Tip

The professional conduct of licensed attorneys in Texas on or after January 1, 1990, is governed by the Texas Disciplinary Rules of Professional Conduct, which were promulgated by the Texas Supreme Court on October 17, 1989. These rules are located at Article X, Section 9 of the State Bar Rules and reprinted as Appendix A to Title 2, Subtitle G of the Texas Government Code in *Vernon's Texas Codes Annotated.*

Cite the Texas Disciplinary Rules of Professional Conduct with the title ("Tex. Disciplinary Rules Prof'l Conduct") followed by a rule number. In the initial citation to this rule, indicate the location of the rule in the Texas Government Code Annotated. A parenthetical indicating the location of the Texas Disciplinary Rules within the State Bar Rules ("Tex. State Bar R.") may be added, if needed for clarity:

Tex. Disciplinary Rules Prof'l Conduct R. 1.02(a)(2), *reprinted in* Tex. Gov't Code Ann., tit. 2, subtit. G, app. A (Tex. State Bar R. art. X, § 9).

17.2.1 Short Form

Subsequent citations of disciplinary rules are by rule number:

Tex. Disciplinary Rules Prof'l Conduct R. 1.02(a)(2).

17.2.2 Comments

The Texas Disciplinary Rules of Professional Conduct are accompanied by comments prepared by the Model Rules Committee of the State Bar of Texas. A comment is first cited according to **Rule 17.2** followed by the abbreviation "cmt." and subsequently cited according to **Rule 17.2.1**:

Tex. Disciplinary Rules Prof'l Conduct R. 4.03 cmt, *reprinted in* Tex. Gov't Code Ann., tit. 2, subtit. G, app. A.

Tex. Disciplinary Rules Prof'l Conduct R. 4.03 cmt.

If a comment is numbered, indicate the comment number immediately following "cmt.":

Tex. Disciplinary Rules Prof'l Conduct R, 8.04 cmt. 6.

If both the rule and the comment are being cited, cite the rule followed by an ampersand and the abbreviation "cmt.":

Tex. Disciplinary Rules Prof'l Conduct R. 4.03 & cmt.

Tex. Disciplinary Rules Prof'l Conduct R. 8.04 & cmt. 6.

17.2.3 Preamble and Terminology Section

The Texas Disciplinary Rules of Professional Conduct includes both a preamble and terminology section. A citation to one of these sections is made according to **Rule 17.2**, with the word "preamble" or "terminology" appended. Citations to the preamble must indicate specific paragraph(s), if applicable:

Tex. Disciplinary Rules Prof'l Conduct preamble ¶¶ 3, 4, *reprinted in* Tex. Gov't Code Ann., tit. 2, subtit. G, app. A.

Tex. Disciplinary Rules Prof'l Conduct terminology, *reprinted in* Tex. Gov't Code Ann., tit. 2, subtit. G, app. A.

Subsequent citations follow **Rule 17.2.1**:

Tex. Disciplinary Rules Prof'l Conduct terminology.

17.3 Ethics Opinions

► Practice Tip

Since 1982, responsibility for issuing ethics opinions has rested with the Committee on Professional Ethics, appointed by the Texas Supreme Court.

Cite ethics opinions from the Texas Committee on Professional Ethics by title ("Tex. Comm. on Prof'l Ethics") and opinion number. Include a reference to the *Texas Bar Journal* ("Tex. B.J.")—including the volume, the page on which the opinion begins, and the exact page of the cited text—if the Committee's opinion appeared therein. Finally, include a parenthetical with the year the opinion was issued:

Tex. Comm. on Prof'l Ethics, Op. 593, 73 Tex. B.J. 254, 255 (2010).

17.4 Texas Rules of Disciplinary Procedure

▸ Practice Tip

The Texas Supreme Court promulgated the Texas Rules of Disciplinary Procedure in 1991. These rules are reprinted in *Vernon's Texas Codes Annotated* as Appendix A-1 to Title 2, Subtitle G of the Texas Government Code.

Cite a rule of the Texas Rules of Disciplinary Procedure by title ("Tex. Rules Disciplinary P.") and rule number. In the initial citation to this rule, indicate the location of the rule in the Texas Government Code Annotated:

Tex. Rules Disciplinary P. R. 2.16(A), *reprinted in* Tex. Gov't Code Ann., tit. 2, subtit. G, app. A-1.

17.4.1 Short Form

Subsequent citations to the Texas Rules of Disciplinary Procedure are by rule number:

Tex. Rules Disciplinary P. R. 2.16(A).

17.5 Texas Code of Judicial Conduct

▸ Practice Tip

The Texas Code of Judicial Conduct was adopted as revised by the Texas Supreme Court in 1993. It is reprinted in *Vernon's Texas Codes Annotated* as Appendix B to Title 2, Subtitle G of the Texas Government Code.

Cite a Canon of the Texas Code of Judicial Conduct by title ("Tex. Code Jud. Conduct") and Canon number. In the initial citation to this rule, indicate the location of the rule in the Texas Government Code Annotated:

Tex. Code Jud. Conduct, Canon 2(A), *reprinted in* Tex. Gov't Code Ann., tit. 2, subtit. G, app. B.

17.5.1 Short Form

Subsequent citations to the Texas Code of Judicial Conduct are by Canon number:

Tex. Code Jud. Conduct, Canon 5.

17.5.2 Advisory Opinions

(a) **Initial Citation.** Advisory opinions on the Texas Code of Judicial Conduct rendered by the Judicial Section of the State Bar's Committee on Judicial Ethics should be cited by the name of the committee ("Comm. on Jud. Ethics"), the author ("State Bar of Tex."), the opinion number, and a parenthetical indicating the year of the opinion. In the initial citation, a parallel citation to the *Texas Judicial System Annual Report* ("Tex. Jud. Council & Off. Ct. Admin. Tex. Jud. Sys. Ann. Rep."), published jointly by the Texas Judicial Council and the Office of Court Administration, must be included:

Comm. on Jud. Ethics, State Bar of Tex., Op. 139 (1991), *reprinted in* 63 Tex. Jud. Council & Off. Ct. Admin. Tex. Jud. Sys. Ann. Rep. 121 (1991).

(b) **Short Form.** Subsequent citations may omit the parallel citation to the *Texas Judicial System Annual Report*:

Comm. on Jud. Ethics, State Bar of Tex., Op. 139.

17.6 Rules for the Removal or Retirement of Judges

▸ Practice Tip

The Rules for the Removal or Retirement of Judges govern proceedings before the State Commission on Judicial Conduct, the Texas Special Court of Review, and the Texas Review Tribunal. The rules can be found in West's *Texas Rules of Court: State.*

Cite the rule with the title ("Tex. Rules Rem'l/Ret. Judg.") and rule number in West's *Texas Rules of Court: State.* Cite as follows:

Tex. Rules Rem'l/Ret. Judg. R. 4(a).

17.7 Rules Governing Admission to the Bar of Texas

If in force, cite the Rules Governing Admission to the Bar of Texas with the title ("Tex. Rules Govern. Bar Adm'n") and rule number in West's *Texas Rules of Court: State.* Cite as follows:

Tex. Rules Govern. Bar Adm'n R. IV(b).

17.7.1 Repealed or Amended Rules

Cite repealed or amended rules by rule number according to **Rule 17.7**, but indicate parenthetically the exact date of promulgation and the exact date of the most recent change:

Tex. R. Govern. Bar Adm'n R. II (June 30, 1992), *amended eff.* Feb. 1, 1994, *amended eff.* Dec. 3, 1997.

PART VI
SECONDARY MATERIAL

18 Books

18.1 Books

For complete citation rules see *The Bluebook* Rule 15 for books and Rule 3.1(c) for supplements. Citations of frequently cited Texas books should include: volume, if more than one; author; title; page or section number; edition, if more than one; and date of publication:

20 Robert W. Hamilton, *Texas Practice Series: Business Organizations* § 26.11 (2d ed. 2004).

1 Steven Goode et al., *Texas Practice Series: Guide to the Texas Rules of Evidence* § 402.3 (2011–2012 ed.).

William V. Dorsaneo III et al., *Texas Civil Procedure: Pretrial Litigation* § 4.01 (2011–2012 ed.).

18.1.1 Books Edited by the Texas Law Review Association

When the Texas Law Review Association is the editor of a publication, Texas is not abbreviated:

Texas Rules of Form: The Greenbook 18.1.1 (Texas Law Review Ass'n ed., 15th ed. 2022).

Texas Law Review Manual on Usage & Style 6.8 (Texas Law Review Ass'n ed., 15th ed. 2020).

18.1.2 *Texas Litigation Guide*

Cite the *Texas Litigation Guide* by the authors of the particular volume:

2 William V. Dorsaneo III, *Texas Litigation Guide* § 21.109[1] (2013).

10 William V. Dorsaneo III et al., *Texas Litigation Guide* § 153.02[1][a] (2013).

18.2 Encyclopedias

Cite encyclopedias by volume, topic, section, and date:

2 Tex. Jur. 3d *Act of God* § 12 (2012).

18.3 Essays, Theses, and Collections

Cite essays compiled in book form by author of the essay, title of essay, editor of the book, volume number, title of book, page numbers or other locator in the book, and date of publication:

Catherine Greene Burnett & Matthew Paul, *Post-Decision Appellate Practice: Motions for Rehearing in the Court of Appeals and Petitions for Discretionary Review, in* State Bar of Tex., 1 *Texas Criminal Appellate Manual,* at F (1996).

18.3.1 Previously Published Materials

Previously published articles or essays reprinted in a collection may contain a parallel citation to the collection:

Alex W. Albright, *The Texas Discovery Privileges: A Fool's Game?,* 70 Texas L. Rev. 781 (1992), *reprinted in Texas Litigation Reader* 28 (A.F. Brooke II & Gregory S. Coleman eds., 1992).

18.3.2 Unpublished Manuscripts and Theses

Cite unpublished manuscripts and theses in roman type, under *The Bluebook* Rule 17. Indicate parenthetically any information that will help locate the source:

William Wabash, Due Process Under the Texas DTPA: Constitutional Limitations 27 (Aug. 14, 2005) (unpublished manuscript) (on file with The University of Texas at Austin, Tarlton Law Library).

Michael G. Henry, Making Sausage in the Zoetrope: Constitutional Limits on Legislative Procedure and State Constitutional Law 92 (Apr. 23, 2002) (unpublished essay) (on file with the author).

18.4 Form Books

Cite form books under *The Bluebook* Rule 15:

Comm. on Pattern Jury Charges, State Bar of Tex., *Texas Pattern Jury Charges: Business* PJC 106.1 (2012).

5 *Texas Forms* § 85:21 (Jason Pariseau ed., 2007 & Supp. 2013).

6 William B. Burford, *West's Texas Forms: Minerals, Oil & Gas* § 3.4 (4th ed. 2008).

4 *Texas Jurisprudence Pleading and Practice Forms* § 66.16 (Jared L. Kronenberg ed., 2d ed. 2012).

7 Michael J. McCormick et al., *Texas Practice: Texas Criminal Forms and Trial Manual* § 44.8 (11th ed. 2005).

19 Conference and Institute Proceedings

19.1 Bound Material

Cite bound conference and institute proceedings in accordance with *The Bluebook* Rule 16.7.7:

Jay L. Westbrook, *Bankruptcy*, 2 Univ. Tex. Mortgage Lending Inst. 10-1 (1986).

19.2 Material from the State Bar of Texas's Professional Development Program

Citations to materials from the State Bar of Texas's Professional Development Program must include the author, title, volume, name of the source ("State Bar of Tex. Prof. Dev. Program"), name of the program and the specific topic, followed by a parenthetical indicating the year of publication:

Heidi Bruegel Cox, *Termination and Adoption*, 2 State Bar of Tex. Prof. Dev. Program, Advanced Family Law Course 36, 36.1 (2005).

19.3 Papers or Essays in a Special Series

Cite papers or essays in a special series of bound material by the volume's title:

Carol S. Carroll, *Small Business Buy and Sell Agreement Forms, in* 58 Tex. Inst. Tax Conf. 177 (2003).

Diane F. Hicks & David G. Hulme, *The Problem of the Small Tract Under Spacing Regulations, in* 107 Tex. Bus. Ass'n Proc. 157 (2005).

Appendices

Appendix A

Case Citation Formats—*Texas Reports* Cases (1846 to 1886) and Republic of Texas Information

A.1 *Texas Reports*—1846 to 1886

▸ Practice Tip

Cases decided between 1867 and 1873 are usually considered less authoritative than those decided earlier or later. From 1867 to 1870, the Texas Supreme Court (then known as the Military Court) was composed of justices appointed by the military commander of Texas during Reconstruction. The decisions of the Military Court (volumes 30–33 of the *Texas Reports*) lacked Texas constitutional basis and are generally not given precedential weight.

From 1870 to 1873, the Texas Supreme Court (then known as the Semicolon Court) sat by authority of the Constitution of 1869, and therefore its decisions (volumes 33–39 of the *Texas Reports*) are valid precedent. Their authoritativeness, however, has occasionally been disparaged.

Cases decided before 1886 do not appear in the *South Western Reporter*. Thus, citation to cases decided between 1846 and 1886 will contain only the *Texas Reports* citation:

Mitchell v. Vickers, 20 Tex. 377, 378 (1857).

Some cases decided in the late 1860s and early 1870s do not carry an actual year of decision. They must instead be cited to the appropriate term, which began in December and ran into the following year:

Fox v. Woods, 35 Tex. 220, 220 (1870–1871).

Cases appearing in the volume 25 supplement to the *Texas Reports* should be cited as:

H. Runge & Co. v. Wyatt, 25 Tex. 291, 292 (Supp. 1860).

Although probably useful only to legal historians, a parallel citation for Civil War conscript cases decided from 1862–1865 may be provided to Charles L. Robards's *Synopses of the Decisions of the Supreme Court of the State of Texas*:

Ex parte Coupland, 26 Tex. 386, 387, Robards 5, 6 (1862).

A few of these cases never appeared in the *Texas Reports* and must be cited to Robards:

Ex parte Randle, Robards 10, 11 (Tex. 1863).

A.2 The Republic of Texas—1840 to 1845

Cases decided by the Supreme Court of the Republic of Texas between 1840 and 1844 are reported in Dallam's *Digest of the Laws of Texas*, a one-volume reporter. When citing Dallam, use the 1845 printing, not the 1881 or subsequent reprints, because pagination in later printings varies from the original 1845 version:

Republic v. McCulloch, Dallam 357, 357 (Tex. 1840).

The cases from the 1845 term of the Supreme Court of the Republic of Texas were unpublished until 1986, when they were published in the *Texas Law Review* Sesquicentennial Special Issue, *The Missing Cases of the Republic of Texas Supreme Court Term, 1845*. Cite as:

Lamar v. Houston (Tex. 1845), 65 Texas L. Rev. 382, 383 (Paulsen rep. 1986).

Appendix B

Court of Appeals—1876 to 1892

The Court of Appeals of the State of Texas was created by the Constitution of 1876 and given appellate jurisdiction in all criminal cases and a few civil cases. Only the opinions in criminal cases were officially reported. In 1892, its civil jurisdiction was removed, and it was renamed the Court of Criminal Appeals.

B.1 Criminal Cases

B.1.1 *Texas Court of Appeals Reports*

Opinions in criminal cases appeared in a separate set of reports begun by the State for criminal cases, the *Texas Court of Appeals Reports* (officially entitled *Cases Argued and Adjudged in the Court of Appeals of the State of Texas*). Cite cases from this reporter as follows, omitting the court designation in the date parenthetical as redundant:

Reynolds v. State, 14 Tex. Ct. App. 427, 428 (1883).

B.1.2 Parallel Citations to the *South Western Reporter*

Citations to some cases in volume 21 and all cases in subsequent volumes of the *Texas Court of Appeals Reports* should contain a parallel citation to the *South Western Reporter*:

Martin v. State, 21 Tex. Ct. App. 1, 10, 17 S.W. 430, 431 (1886).

Although citation to the *Texas Court of Appeals Reports* is preferred, the source may not be readily available. If the *Texas Court of Appeals Reports* is unavailable, cite the *South Western Reporter* only and parenthetically note the jurisdictional designation "Tex. Ct. App." along with the year of decision. The following form is also acceptable:

Martin v. State, 17 S.W. 430, 431 (Tex. Ct. App. 1886).

B.2 Civil Cases

The few civil cases decided by the old Texas Court of Appeals were privately reported, first by Judges White and Willson and later by Judge Willson alone. The cases are found in the four-volume set of *Condensed Reports of Decisions in Civil Causes in the Court of Appeals*. Volume 1 should be cited as "White & W." Volumes 2 through 4 should be cited as "Willson":

Gibbons v. Braden, 1 White & W. 128, 129 (Tex. Ct. App. 1883).

Watson v. Cox, 2 Willson 209, 210 (Tex. Ct. App. 1884).

Sole or parallel citation to the *South Western Reporter* should be provided for cases appearing in volume 4 of Willson:

Durie v. Anderson, 16 S.W. 345, 346, 4 Willson 432, 433 (Tex. Ct. App. 1891).

Appendix C

Commission of Appeals—1879 to 1892

C.1 1881 to 1892

Beginning in 1881, the Texas Supreme Court and the Texas Court of Appeals could transfer cases to the Texas Commission of Appeals without the parties' consent. The Commission's opinions in cases referred by the Texas Court of Appeals were not published.[1]

C.1.1 Adopted Commission Decisions

Cases transferred to the Commission of Appeals by the Texas Supreme Court without the parties' consent were published in either the *Texas Reports*, the *South Western Reporter*, or both. The Commission's decisions in these cases were adopted by the Court and should be cited according to **Rule 2.3.1**, **Rule 2.3.2**, **Rule 5.2.2**, and **Appendix A.1**:

Dwyer v. Olivari, 16 S.W. 800, 801 (Tex. [Comm'n Op.] 1891).

Burck v. Burroughs, 64 Tex. 445, 447 (1885).

Pardue v. James, 74 Tex. 299, 302, 12 S.W. 1, 2 (1889).

C.1.2 Unadopted Commission Decisions

Cases transferred to the Commission by the Texas Supreme Court from 1881 to 1884 with the parties' consent were published in Posey's *Texas Unreported Cases*. The Court did not adopt those decisions, and they do not serve as precedent. These cases should be attributed to the Texas Commission of Appeals according to **Appendix C.2**.

---

1. Professor Baade's history of the Texas Supreme Court in the Reconstruction Era discusses this Commission of Appeals. *See* Hans W. Baade, *Chapters in the History of the Supreme Court of Texas: Reconstruction and Redemption (1866–1882)*, 40 St. Mary's L.J. 17, 24, 31–32 (2008).

Some opinions in volume 2 of Posey's reports were published without a specific date. Cite these cases by giving an approximate date parenthetically:

Litton v. Thompson, 2 Posey 577, 578 (Tex. Comm'n App. between 1882 and 1884) (not precedential).

C.2 1879 to 1881

Before 1881, the Texas Supreme Court and the Texas Court of Appeals could refer cases to the Texas Commission of Appeals only with the parties' consent. The Commission's actions determined the outcome of the particular case and did not serve as precedent. Further, the State lacked statutory authorization to publish these opinions. These decisions were included in two private reporters: Posey's *Texas Unreported Cases* and White and Willson's *Condensed Reports of Decisions in Civil Causes in the Court of Appeals.*

C.2.1 Cases from the Texas Supreme Court

Posey's two-volume compilation contains opinions of cases referred to the Commission by the parties' consent from the Texas Supreme Court.[2] When citing these decisions include the title, volume number, reporter ("Posey"), first page of the decision, exact page on which the cited material appears, a date parenthetical including the court's name ("Tex. Comm'n App.), and a precedential value parenthetical:

Mitchell v. Nix, 1 Posey 126, 135 (Tex. Comm'n App. 1880) (not precedential).

2. J.W. Posey, *Texas Unreported Cases* (St. Louis, Gilbert Book Co. 1891); 1 S.A. Posey, *Texas Unreported Cases* (St. Louis, Gilbert Book Co. 1886). Some copies of volume two list Vernon Law Book Co. in Kansas City as the publisher.

C.2.2 Cases from the Texas Court of Appeals

Volume 1 of White and Willson's reports contains abridged opinions of cases referred to the Commission by the parties' consent from the Texas Court of Appeals. Cite these decisions per **Rule C.2.1**, but with the proper reporter title ("White & W."):

Stringfellow v. Thomson, 1 White & W. 565, 566 (Tex. Comm'n App. 1881) (not precedential).

Appendix D[1]

Table of Notations Used on Petitions for Review in the Texas Supreme Court—September 1, 1997 to Present

Notation	Defining Statute or Rule
Petition denied [pet. denied] The Texas Supreme Court is not satisfied that the opinion of the court of appeals has correctly declared the law in all respects but determines that the petition presents no error that requires reversal or that is of such importance to the jurisprudence of the State as to require correction.	**Tex. R. App. P. 56.1(b)(1)**
Petition refused [pet. ref'd] The Texas Supreme Court determines—after a response has been filed or requested—that the judgment of the court of appeals is correct and the legal principles announced in the opinion are likewise correct. The opinion of the court of appeals has the same precedential value as an opinion of the Texas Supreme Court.	**Tex. R. App. P. 56.1(c)**

1. Much of the information contained in this chart, provided by Associate Dean James Hambleton of the Texas Wesleyan University School of Law, was published in the September 2002 issue of the *Texas Bar Journal* and is reprinted here with permission. *See* James Hambleton, *Notations for Subsequent Histories in Civil Cases*, 65 Tex. B.J. 694 (2002).

Table of Notations Used on Petitions for Review

Notation	Defining Statute or Rule
Petition struck [pet. struck] The Texas Supreme Court has not reviewed the merits of the appeal, but has struck the petition for failure to comply with court rules, and has either required the petitioner to revise the petition or has chosen to consider the case without allowing the petition to be revised.	**Tex. R. App. P. 53.9**
Petition dismissed [pet. dism'd] The Texas Supreme Court can dismiss a petition for failure to follow any of the rules of procedure. The Texas Supreme Court has not reviewed the merits of the appeal.	***See* Tex. R. App. P. 60.6**
Petition granted and judgment vacated without reference to the merits [pet. granted, judgm't vacated w.r.m.] If the parties settle, on the joint motion of the parties the Texas Supreme Court may grant the petition for review and, without considering the merits, render a judgment to effectuate the agreement. It may alternatively remand the cause to the trial court for rendition of judgment in accordance with the parties' settlement agreement. The Court may dispose of a severable portion of the proceeding if it will not prejudice the remaining parties. The opinion of the court of appeals is not vacated and has the precedential value of a petition dismissed case.	**Tex. R. App. P. 56.3**
Petition dismissed by agreement of the parties [pet. dism'd by agr.] By motion of the parties, a petition can be dismissed by agreement.	**Tex. R. App. P. 42.1(a)(2)**

Notation	Defining Statute or Rule
Petition granted [pet. granted] At least four justices are convinced that the court of appeals erred in its judgment.	**N/A[2]**
Petition dismissed for want of jurisdiction [pet. dism'd w.o.j.] The Texas Supreme Court lacks jurisdiction to consider the petition.	**Tex. R. App. P. 56.1(b)(2)**
Petition withdrawn [pet. withdrawn] The petitioner by motion may request the petition be withdrawn. The grant of the motion results in the petition's withdrawal. The Texas Supreme Court has not reviewed the merits of the appeal.	**Tex. R. App. P. 42.1(a)(1)**
Petition abated [pet. abated] A bankruptcy suspends the appeal. The Texas Supreme Court has not reviewed the merits of the appeal, but may do so if the petition is reinstated.	**Tex. R. App. P. 8.2**

2. The Clerk of the Court for the Texas Supreme Court publishes a guide to the internal procedures of the Court. Available on the website for the Clerk's office, it not only contains information on the Court's voting practices for granting review, but on a whole host of topics related to practicing before the Court. *See generally* Blake A. Hawthorne, *Supreme Court of Texas: Internal Operating Procedures* (2013).

Table of Notations Used on Petitions for Review

Notation	Defining Statute or Rule
Petition filed [pet. filed] The petition has been timely filed, but the Court has taken no action on it. (With some exceptions, to be timely filed a petition must be filed within 45 days of either the date the court of appeals rendered judgment or the date of the court of appeals' last disposition of a motion for rehearing or reconsideration en banc.) The Texas Supreme Court has not reviewed the merits of the appeal.	***See* Tex. R. App. P. 53.7**
Petition pending [pet. pending] A petition has been timely filed, and the Texas Supreme Court has ordered briefing on the merits but has not yet granted the petition or rendered a judgment. The Court may order briefing on the merits with or without granting the petition for review.	***See* Tex. R. App. P. 53.7, 55.1**
No petition history [no pet. h.] No petition has been filed, but the time for filing has not yet run. (With some exceptions, to be timely filed a petition must be filed within 45 days of either the date the court of appeals rendered judgment or the date of the court of appeals' last disposition of a motion for rehearing or en banc reconsideration.) The Texas Supreme Court has not reviewed the merits of the appeal.	***See* Tex. R. App. P. 53.7(a)**
No petition [no pet.] No petition has been filed, and the time for filing has expired. (With some exceptions, to be timely filed a petition must be filed within 45 days of either the date the court of appeals rendered judgment or the date of the court of appeals' last disposition of a motion for rehearing or en banc reconsideration.) The Texas Supreme Court has not reviewed the merits of the appeal.	***See* Tex. R. App. P. 53.7(a)**

Appendix E

Table of Notations Pertaining to Writs of Error in the Texas Supreme Court—Before September 1, 1997

Notation	Date
No writ [no writ] Neither party filed an application for writ of error to the Texas Supreme Court.	**9/1/1892 to 8/31/1997**
Writ dismissed by agreement [writ dism'd by agr.] Writ was dismissed by agreement of the parties. The precedential value of such cases is equivalent to a "writ dismissed" case. *See Hous. Cable TV, Inc. v. Inwood W. Civic Ass'n*, 860 S.W.2d 72, 73 & n.3 (Tex. 1993).	**3/1/1939 to 8/31/1997**
Writ dismissed [writ dism'd]	**3/1/1939[1] to 8/31/1997**
Writ dismissed for want of jurisdiction [writ dism'd w.o.j.] The Texas Supreme Court lacks jurisdiction to consider the application.	

1. The Texas Supreme Court has designated applications for a writ of error "writ dismissed" since September 1, 1892. The current meaning of this designation, however, did not solidify until March 1, 1939. Prior to 1939, its exact meaning fluctuated.

For complete guidance on interpreting "writ dismissed," see Justice Gordon Simpson, *Notations on Applications for Writs of Error*, 12 Tex. B.J. 547, 570–75 (1949). Then-Justice, later-Chief Justice, Joe Greenhill provides another concise summary of this history in his *Uniform Citations for Briefs: With Observations on the Meanings of the Stamps or Markings Used in Denying Writs of Error*, 27 Tex. B.J. 323, 386–88 (1964).

Table of Notations Pertaining to Writs of Error

Notation	Date
Writ dismissed, judgment correct [writ dism'd judgm't cor.] In cases within the jurisdiction of the Texas Supreme Court, the judgment is correct but the Texas Supreme Court is not satisfied that the opinion of the court of appeals in all respects has correctly declared the law.	**3/1/1939 to 9/1/1941**
Writ refused for want of merit [writ ref'd w.o.m.] Judgment of court of civil appeals is correct but the Texas Supreme Court is not satisfied that the opinion in all respects has correctly declared the law.	**9/1/1941 to 2/1/1946**
Writ refused, no reversible error [writ ref'd n.r.e.] The Texas Supreme Court is not satisfied that the opinion of the court of civil appeals in all respects has correctly declared the law but is of the opinion that the application presents no error that is reversible.	**2/1/1946 to 12/31/1987**
Writ denied [writ denied] The Texas Supreme Court is not satisfied that the opinion of the court of appeals has correctly declared the law but is of the opinion that the application presents no error that requires reversal or is of such importance to the jurisprudence of the State as to require correction.	**1/1/1988 to 8/31/1997**

Notation	Date
Writ refused [writ ref'd] Judgment of the court of civil appeals is correct and the Texas Supreme Court is satisfied that the opinion has correctly declared the law. Such cases have equal precedential value with the Texas Supreme Court's own opinions.	**6/14/1927[2] to 8/31/1997**
Writ granted without reference to merits [writ granted w.r.m.] If the parties settle, on the parties' joint motion the Texas Supreme Court may grant the application for writ of error, set aside the judgments of the court of appeals and the trial court without reference to the merits, and remand the cause to the trial court for rendition of judgment in accordance with the settlement of the parties. The opinion of the court of appeals is not vacated and has the precedential value of a writ dismissed case.	**11/11/1992 to 8/31/1997**
Writ granted [writ granted] At least four justices are convinced that the court of appeals erred in its judgment. Prior to this date, the Supreme Court granted the writ if three justices voted to do so.	**1/15/1988[3] to 8/31/1997**

2. The Texas Supreme Court has designated applications for a writ of error "writ refused" since September 1, 1892. The current meaning of this designation, however, did not solidify until June 14, 1927. Prior to 1927, it did not always signify agreement with the lower court's judgment.

For complete guidance on interpreting "writ refused," see Justice Gordon Simpson, *Notations on Applications for Writs of Error*, 12 Tex. B.J. 547, 572–75 (1949). Then-Justice, later-Chief Justice, Joe Greenhill provides another concise summary of this history in his *Uniform Citations for Briefs: With Observations on the Meanings of the Stamps or Markings Used in Denying Writs of Error*, 27 Tex. B.J. 323, 386–88 (1964).

3. *See* Elaine A. Carlson & Roland Garcia, Jr., *Discretionary Review Powers of the Texas Supreme Court*, 50 Tex. B.J. 1201, 1202 & n.21 (1987). It appears that, although it was approved for publication, the Supreme Court's order establishing this change in procedure was never in fact published.

Appendix F

Table of Notations Used on Petitions for Review in the Court of Criminal Appeals

Notation	Defining Statute or Rule
No Petition History [no pet. h.] No petition has been filed, and the time for filing has not yet run (generally within 30 days after either the day that the court of appeals' judgment was rendered or the day the last timely motion for rehearing or for reconsideration en banc was denied by the court of appeals). The Court of Criminal Appeals has not reviewed the merits of the appeal.	***See* Tex. R. App. P. 68.2**
No Petition [no pet.] No petition has been filed, and the time for filing has expired. The Court of Criminal Appeals has not reviewed the merits of the appeal.	***See* Tex. R. App. P. 68.2**
Petition Filed [pet. filed] The petition has been timely filed, but the Court of Criminal Appeals has taken no action on it. The Court of Criminal Appeals has not reviewed the merits of the appeal.	***See* Tex. R. App. P. 68.2, 69**

Notation	Defining Statute or Rule
Petition Dismissed [pet. dism'd] A petition will be dismissed if five judges believe that discretionary review should not have been granted after discretionary review was previously granted.	**Tex. R. App. P. 69.3**
Petition Refused, Untimely Filed [pet. ref'd, untimely filed] The Court of Criminal Appeals may summarily refuse a petition that does not comply with the Texas Rules of Appellate Procedure, including the relevant time limits.	***See* Tex. R. App. P. 68.6**
Petition Refused [pet. ref'd] If the petition does not receive the vote of four judges for discretionary review, the petition will be refused.	**Tex. R. App. P. 69.1**
Petition Granted [pet. granted] Discretionary review will be granted if four judges vote for the petition. Use this designation only when the Court of Criminal Appeals has granted the petition but has issued no other disposition of the case, on the merits or otherwise.	**Tex. R. App. P. 69.1**
Review Granted, Without Petition [rev. granted, without pet.] The Court of Criminal Appeals may grant discretionary review with the vote of four judges in the absence of a petition at any time before the mandate of the court of appeals issues.	**Tex. R. App. P. 67.1**

Appendix G
Prior Constitutions

G.1 Prior Constitutions of the State of Texas

Always include the date of adoption when citing a Texas constitution that has been totally superseded—the constitutions of 1845, 1861, 1866, and 1869:

Tex. Const. of 1869, art. III, § 3.

If the cited provision was added after the constitution was adopted, indicate the date of its addition parenthetically:

Tex. Const. of 1869, art. V, § 4 (1873).

Prior constitutions are reprinted in volume three of *Vernon's Annotated Constitution of the State of Texas* and in H.P.N. Gammel's ten-volume *The Laws of Texas 1822–1897*. It is unnecessary, however, to include a parallel citation to either of those sources.

G.2 Constitutional Convention Ordinances

Ordinances adopted by a Texas constitutional convention prior to 1886 carried the same weight as constitutional provisions. Gammel reprints these ordinances in full, while volume three of *Vernon's Annotated Constitution of the State of Texas* includes only selected provisions. Ordinances should be cited to Gammel:

Tex. Ord. no. 11, § 7 (Mar. 30, 1866), *reprinted in* 5 H.P.N. Gammel, *The Laws of Texas 1822–1897*, at 895, 897 (Austin, Gammel Book Co. 1898).

G.3 Constitution of the Republic of Texas

The constitution of the Republic of Texas should be cited to H.P.N. Gammel's *The Laws of Texas 1822–1897*, although it is also reprinted in volume three of *Vernon's Annotated Constitution of the State of Texas*:

Repub. Tex. Const. of 1836, art. III, § 1, *reprinted in* 1 H.P.N. Gammel, *The Laws of Texas 1822–1897*, at 1069, 1073 (Austin, Gammel Book Co. 1898).

G.4 Constitution of the State of Coahuila and Texas

Prior to existing as the Republic of Texas, Texas was part of a Mexican state named Coahuila and Texas (sometimes called Coahuila y Tejas). The 1827 constitution of Coahuila and Texas should be cited to H.P.N. Gammel's *The Laws of Texas 1822–1897*:

Coahuila & Tex. Const. of 1827, art. XX, § 2, *reprinted in* 1 H.P.N. Gammel, *The Laws of Texas 1822–1897*, at 423, 425 (Austin, Gammel Book Co. 1898).

▸ Practice Tip

Although H.P.N. Gammel's compilation of nineteenth-century Texas legal materials was published over a century ago, it remains an important source for many legal materials relating to early Texas history, from colonial times through early statehood.

The University of North Texas has created a free-to-the-public, digital scan of Gammel, which is available on its website.

Appendix H

Texas Statutes and Current Rules—Abbreviations

H.1 Subject Matter Codes

Code	Abbreviation
Agriculture	Tex. Agric. Code
Alcoholic Beverage	Tex. Alco. Bev. Code
Business and Commerce	Tex. Bus. & Com. Code
Business Organizations	Tex. Bus. Orgs. Code
Civil Practice and Remedies	Tex. Civ. Prac. & Rem. Code
Education	Tex. Educ. Code
Election	Tex. Elec. Code
Estates	Tex. Est. Code
Family	Tex. Fam. Code
Finance	Tex. Fin. Code
Government	Tex. Gov't Code
Health and Safety	Tex. Health & Safety Code
Human Resources	Tex. Hum. Res. Code
Insurance	Tex. Ins. Code
Labor	Tex. Lab. Code
Local Government	Tex. Loc. Gov't Code
Natural Resources	Tex. Nat. Res. Code
Occupations	Tex. Occ. Code
Parks and Wildlife	Tex. Parks & Wild. Code
Penal	Tex. Penal Code
Property	Tex. Prop. Code
Special District Local Laws	Tex. Spec. Dist. Code
Tax	Tex. Tax Code
Transportation	Tex. Transp. Code
Utilities	Tex. Util. Code
Water	Tex. Water Code

H.2 Independent Codes

Code	Abbreviation
Criminal Procedure	Tex. Code Crim. Proc.
Insurance	Tex. Ins. Code
Probate	Tex. Prob. Code
Business Corporations	Tex. Bus. Corp. Act

H.3 Current Rules

Rules	Abbreviation
Rules of Civil Procedure	Tex. R. Civ. P.
Rules of Judicial Administration	Tex. R. Jud. Admin.
Rules of Appellate Procedure	Tex. R. App. P.
Rules of Evidence	Tex. R. Evid.
State Bar Rules	Tex. State Bar R.
Disciplinary Rules of Professional Conduct	Tex. Disciplinary Rules Prof'l Conduct
Rules of Disciplinary Procedure	Tex. Rules Disciplinary P.
Code of Judicial Conduct	Tex. Code Jud. Conduct
Rules for the Removal or Retirement of Judges	Tex. Rules Rem'l/Ret. Judg.
Rules Governing Admission to the Bar	Tex. Rules Govern. Bar Adm'n

Appendix I

Dates of Pre-1876 Legislative Sessions

Before the enactment of the 1876 constitution, the legislature did not always follow the present system of meeting for one biennial regular session and an indefinite number of specially called sessions. Citation to these legislative sessions may require special designations, such as "Adj. S." for "Adjourned Session," "Prov. S." for "Provisional Session," and "2d R.S." for "Second Regular Session." Citations to session laws from the 1st, 2d, 5th, 7th, 11th, 13th, and 15th Legislatures should simply omit the session designation because these Legislatures met for only one session. The Legislative Reference Library of Texas has further information about all legislative sessions on its website.

For full citation guidance for pre-1876 statutes, see **Rule 11.2**.

Legislature	Date
1st	February 16 to May 13, 1846.
2d	December 13, 1847, to March 20, 1848.
3d	November 5, 1849, to February 11, 1850.
	August 12 to September 6, 1850 — First Called Session.
	November 18 to December 3, 1850 — Second Called Session.
4th	November 3, 1851, to February 16, 1852.
	January 10 to February 7, 1853 — First Called Session.
5th	November 7, 1853, to February 13, 1854.
6th	November 5, 1855, to February 4, 1856.
	July 7 to September 1, 1856 — Adjourned Session.
7th	November 2, 1857, to February 16, 1858.
8th	November 7, 1859, to February 13, 1860.
	January 21 to February 9, 1861 — First Called Session
	March 18 to April 9, 1861 — Adjourned Called Session.
9th	November 4, 1861, to January 14, 1862.
	February 2 to March 7, 1863 — First Called Session.

Legislature	Date
10th	November 2 to December 16, 1863.
	May 9 to May 28, 1864—First Called Session.
	October 17 to November 15, 1864—Second Called Session.
11th	August 6 to November 13, 1866.
12th	February 8 to February 24, 1870—Provisional Session.
	April 26 to August 15, 1870—First Called Session.
	January 10 to May 31, 1871—Regular Session.
	September 12 to December 2, 1871—Adjourned Session.
13th	January 14 to June 4, 1873.
14th	January 13 to May 4, 1874—First Regular Session.
	January 12 to March 15, 1875—Second Regular Session.
15th	April 18 to August 21, 1876.

Appendix J

Chief Justices and Associate Justices of the Texas Courts of Civil Appeals (1892 to 1911)

Judge	District Served	Judge	District Served
Bookhout, J.	Dallas	Lightfoot, H.W.	Dallas
Cobbs, T.D.	San Antonio	McKenzie, J.F.	El Paso
Collard, W.E.	Austin	McMeans, S.A.	Galveston
Conner, T.H.	Fort Worth	Neill, H.H.	San Antonio
Dunklin, Irby	Fort Worth	Peticolas, W.M.	El Paso
Eidson, J.A.	Austin	Pleasants, H. Clay	Galveston
Finley, N.W.	Dallas	Pleasants, R.A.	Galveston
Fisher, H.C.	Austin	Presler, J.M. (1908)	Fort Worth
Fly, W.S.	San Antonio	Presler, J.M. (1911)	Amarillo
Garrett, C.C.	Galveston	Rainey, Anson	Dallas
Gill, W.H.	Galveston	Reese, T.S.	Galveston
Graham, Jas. A.	Amarillo	Rice, B.H.	Austin
Hall, R.W.	Amarillo	Speer, Ocie	Fort Worth
Head, H.O.	Fort Worth	Stephens, I.W.	Fort Worth
Higgins, E.F.	El Paso	Streetman, Sam	Austin
Hodges, Wm.	Texarkana	Talbot, J.M.	Dallas
Hunter, Sam J.	Fort Worth	Tarlton, B.D.	Fort Worth
James, J.H.	San Antonio	Templeton, Howard	Dallas
Jenkins, C.H.	Austin	Williams, F.A.	Galveston
Key, W.M.	Austin	Willson, Samuel P.	Texarkana
Levy, Richard B.	Texarkana		

Appendix K
Rules No Longer in Effect

K.1 Rules of the Republic of Texas and Early State of Texas

Cite the Republic of Texas court rules and early State of Texas court rules to the first volume of the *Texas Reports*, to the *Texas Law Review* Sesquicentennial Special Issue, *Rules of Procedure in Early Texas Courts*, 65 Texas L. Rev. 451 (1986), or both:

Tex. Sup. Ct. R. 1, 1 Tex. 848 (1846), *reprinted in Rules of Procedure in Early Texas Courts*, 65 Texas L. Rev. 451, 453 (1986).

Note any corrections to the rules ("*reprinted as corrected in*"):

Repub. Tex. Sup. Ct. R. 13, 1 Tex. 846–47 (1840), *reprinted as corrected in Rules of Procedure in Early Texas Courts*, 65 Texas L. Rev. 451, 456 (1986).

K.2 Rules of Civil Evidence No Longer in Effect

The Texas Supreme Court promulgated the Texas Rules of Evidence for civil proceedings effective September 1, 1983. These rules were renamed the Texas Rules of Civil Evidence in 1988. Cite as follows:

Tex. R. Civ. Evid. 801(a).

K.3 Rules of Criminal Evidence Adopted in 1985

The Texas Rules of Criminal Evidence, which were adopted in 1985, are cited as follows:

Tex. R. Crim. Evid. 803.

K.4 Former Canons of Ethics, Former Texas Code of Professional Responsibility, and Other Rules No Longer in Force

When citing the former Canons of Ethics, Disciplinary Rules, Ethical Considerations of the superseded Code of Professional Responsibility, or to older rules, canons, or opinions, include a citation to the *Texas Bar Journal, South Western Reporter (Texas Cases),* or the State Bar's 1958 *Rules and Canons of Ethics,* if therein, in that order of preference. If not included in one of these sources, give the date of promulgation. A date of repeal or amendment must also be noted parenthetically:

Tex. State Bar R., art. XII, § 8, DR 2-101 (Tex. Code of Prof'l Resp.), 34 Tex. B.J. 757, 758 (1971, superseded 1990).

Comm. on Interpretation of the Canons of Ethics, State Bar of Tex., Op. 1 (1946), *reprinted in* State Bar of Tex., *Rules and Canons of Ethics* 41, 41 (1958).

Index